fresh
HERB
cooking

fresh
HERB
cooking

LINDA DANNENBERG   PHOTOGRAPHS BY ELLEN SILVERMAN

Stewart, Tabori & Chang • New York

PROJECT EDITOR: Sandra Gilbert
PRODUCTION: Pamela Schechter
DESIGNER: Nina Barnett
FOOD STYLIST: Anne Disrude
PROP STYLIST: Betty Alfenito

Published in 2001 by Stewart, Tabori & Chang
A division of Harry N. Abrams
115 West 18th Street
New York, NY 10011

Library of Congress Cataloging-in-Publication Data
Dannenberg, Linda.
Fresh herb cooking / Linda Dannenberg ; photographs by Ellen Silverman.
p. cm.
Includes index.
ISBN 1-58479-061-X
1. Cookery (Herbs) I. Title.

TX819.H4 D26 2001
641.6'57—dc21
2001016223

The text of this book was composed in Clarendon Light and Univers.

Printed in Singapore

1 3 5 7 9 10 8 6 4 2
First Printing

To Steve and to Ben, with love

acknowledgments

I am deeply grateful to all the people who helped make this book a reality. My first thanks go to all the superb chefs and terrific home cooks who so generously contributed their recipes and their expertise: David and Nito Carpita, Mas de Cornud; René, Danièle, and Sandra Bérard, Hostellerie Bérard; Rocco DiSpirito, Union Pacific; Philippe Legendre, Four Seasons Hotel George V; Sue Chapman, The Lodge at Skylonda; the members of the New York Unit of the Herb Society of America, particularly Page Dickey and Maggie Limburg; Hélène Darroze, Restaurant Hélène Darroze; Pierre and Chantal Gagnaire, Restaurant Pierre Gagnaire; Jean-Louis Meteigner, La Cachette; Eric Brennan, The Federalist, Hotel Fifteen Beacon; Denis Jaricot, CuisinArt Resort; Jean-Marc Lappel, Hotel San Régis; Aude Kamlet; Max London, also Michael and Wendy London, Mrs. London's Bakery; John and Michael Scaglio, Scaglio's Marketplace; Benoît Witz, Hostellerie de l'Abbaye de La Celle; Marc Marchand, Hotel Meurice; Oliver Dudler, Peninsula Hotel, New York; Charlene Rollins, Little Sammy's Cowboy Bistro; Christopher Freeman, The Wauwinet; Jérôme Fessard, Hotel Lancaster; Barbara Fenner, The Menemsha Galley; Wolfgang and Claire Pinkwart, Hotel Mont Cervin, Tim Barger, Swissôtel-The Watergate Hotel; Anne and Fabrice Néel, Château Lamothe; James Staiano, New York Palace Hotel; Todd Weisz, Turnberry Isle Resort and Club; Nalam Nastili, Le Touessrok Resort and Ile aux Cerfs; Jean-Pierre Court, D'Chez Eux; Didier Schneiter, Beau Rivage Palace Hotel; Pierre Lienard, Pâtisserie Stohrer; Eric Redolat, Lausanne Palace Hotel; and Christian Willer, Hotel Martinez. I would also like to thank Alain Ducasse, Burt Wolf, Catherine Martel of the Four Seasons Hotel George V; Claudia Schall of the Hotel Meurice; Joseph Georges and Sabrina Blanc-Miele of the Hotel San Régis; and Grace Leo-Andrieu and John Petch of the Hotel Lancaster.

I am full of admiration for the work done by my editors and all the excellent staff at Stewart, Tabori & Chang. I would like to express my deep appreciation to publisher Leslie Stoker for enthusiastically taking on this project; to my wonderful editor, Sandy Gilbert, for her patience, understanding, and skill in making this book come to life; to Liana Fredley, tester and copy editor extraordinaire; to Emily Von Kohorn for her yeoman organizational skills; to Nina Barnett for her artistic vision and creative design; and to Pamela Schechter for overseeing the production of this book with great care. For the handsome photographs that enliven this book, I am grateful to photographer Ellen Silverman and her talented staff. I would also like to thank my friends and neighbors who comprise part of the famous Katonah Tart Tasting Committee for their happy participation in the testing and tasting process: Alice Finley, and Teresa and Leslie Scott; and another loyal and enthusiastic tester, Marc Freidus.

As always, I am deeply grateful to my agents, Gayle Benderoff and Deborah Geltman, who work so hard navigating my ideas from concept to contract, and who are wonderful sounding boards and diplomatic counselors all the way through to completion.

contents

introduction

ON A RESTAURANT MENU, in a baker's display case, on the counter of a gourmet take-out shop, dishes with herbs in their names distinguish themselves from the crowd with an almost ineffable appeal. Beyond the anticipated pleasures of the flavor and enticing aroma, herb cuisine evokes images of gardens and countryside, and inspires perceptions of freshness and health, of food rustic and elegantly earthy.

I'VE BEEN COLLECTING AND PREPARING herb recipes for years, using, whenever possible, the herbs I grow in large and small containers around my house. I am always experimenting in the kitchen, playing with herbs when I have an abundance of them. Since with herbs a little goes a long way, there are always more herbs than it is possible to use. And so I continue on my perpetual quest—for more herb recipes, for easier and more practical ways to use herbs and to preserve them through the year. Most home cooks, including myself, usually gather or buy a bunch of herbs to make a single recipe, use a sprig or two, then store the rest in the refrigerator, where it eventually turns black and slimy and then gets tossed out. But, as I've discovered, there are so many ways to use fresh herbs that it's almost a crime to let a beautiful bunch molder away in the fridge.

WHENEVER I TRAVEL, whether I find myself in a modest bistro on a barefoot island, in a small, charming bakery in upstate New York, or in a glamorous three-star restaurant in Paris, I am fascinated by what local chefs are doing with herbs, and always gravitate to the herb-infused item on the menu. This book was inspired by all the unique and innovative ways the chefs I was privileged to meet over the past few years prepare and use herbs. The recipes come from talented home cooks as well as from top chefs from around the world, from the island of Mauritius in the Indian Ocean to the back-country of Oregon.

I'VE FOCUSED EXCLUSIVELY on fresh herbs because, quite simply, fresh herbs are better than the dried variety. Their flavor is truer, deeper, "greener." Although the book features a wide variety of herbs, there is a particular emphasis on the most popular and widely available herbs—what I call my Top Thirteen, detailed below.

The recipes use herbs in many ways—pureed into a thick green sauce; minced and sprinkled on as a garnish; infused in a base ingredient such as milk and then discarded; mashed into an unusual pesto; chopped and mixed in as an essential ingredient; "melted" in butter and then smoothed into a rich sauce; crushed and mixed into a sweet dessert cream filling; and many more.

NOT ONLY WILL HERBS ENHANCE FOODS you prepare yourself, but they improve prepared—frozen or canned—foods, adding a crucial touch of freshness. I know a woman who loves to entertain, but who hates to cook. When guests are coming over, she loads up on cartons of frozen prepared foods, heats them up, and transfers them to an attractive casserole. Then she stirs in a small handful of chopped fresh herbs and a cup or so of red or white wine, heats the mixture for about five minutes, then serves her guests, thinking no one is the wiser. Certainly the food is better than it would be without the herbs and wine!

THE WORLD OF HERBS IS AN INTRIGUING ONE, with a history that goes back almost to the beginning of time. Rue, mint, and cumin are frequently mentioned in the Bible. The Greeks and Romans—writers such as Virgil, Pliny, and Horace—sang the praises of fresh herbs, while one particular Roman bon vivant, connoisseur, and some say libertine—Marcus Apicius—born in the first century, wrote a seminal cookbook featuring herbs, *De re conquinaria libri decem (Cuisine in Ten Books),* which remains a precious reference work two thousand years later. Kings Charlemagne and Louis XIV collected and cultivated herbs in their royal gardens. Casanova and his contemporaries chewed herbs to sweeten their breath. And cooks everywhere, in the days before refrigeration, used herbs, as they did many other flavorings such as curries and other spices, to cover up the rancid taste of spoiled meats. Although herbs have never completely disappeared from the culinary scene, there have been marked ebbs and flows in their use and popularity. In our own recent history, it was in the early 1970s, when the natural and organic movements truly took hold, that interest in fresh herbs returned with a vengeance, and it continues apace to this day. Where once only fresh parsley—usually purchased for use as a garnish—was available in the supermarket produce aisle, today there are usually four or five and sometimes up to ten fresh herbs offered year round. The perfect answer to current dietary concerns, herbs can enrich just about any dish, adding depth of flavor and essential vitamins and minerals without adding any fat, sugar, salt, or artificial chemicals as so many other flavor enhancers do.

the essential herbs

MOST OF THE RECIPES IN THIS BOOK FEATURE A SELECT GROUP of the most available and popular herbs, the essential herbs, the stalwarts. They come from both of the two distinct groups of herbs, the delicate "green herbs," the annuals, such as dill and basil; and the sturdier, heartier "woody herbs," the perennials, such as thyme and rosemary. Below, they comprise my Top-Thirteen List.

Basil: Common sweet basil and its many cousins, such as opal and purple ruffled, Thai, and globe, are some of the most versatile herbs, and are wonderful in salads (particularly in a salad with tomatoes—the vegetable with which it has the greatest affinity—garlic, oil, and vinegar), in butter sauces for fish, and especially in tomato sauces. The spicy, clovelike aroma and flavor of this annual, also characterized by overtones of mint, enhances oils, vinegars, pesto, fruit salads, and even chocolate. In Italy it signifies love; in France it

is called *l'herbe royale,* and is considered the king of herbs; and in India a house surrounded by basil is considered blessed.

Bay: Powerful and pungent, with a distinctive hint of nutmeg and crisp, stiff leaves, bay, or bay laurel as it's sometimes known, is a shrub or small tree that is not particularly easy to grow. Used just a leaf or two at a time, bay is an essential component of a classic bouquet garni, along with thyme and parsley, and is used to season stuffings, stews, soups, chicken, marinades, and a variety of vegetables, among them beets, carrots, eggplant, and potatoes. Always remove it before serving a dish, since the sharp edges of a bay leaf lurking in a stew can get stuck in your throat.

Chives: One of the delicate *fines herbes,* in company with tarragon, parsley, and chervil, chives are a member of the onion family—the subtlest member. They are wonderful in salads and egg dishes (especially omelets), mixed with cream cheese as a spread, with sour cream to top baked potatoes, sprinkled on soups, tossed with potato salads, or mixed into softened butter. A hearty and abundant perennial, chives grow nicely in pots; their little pom-pom flowers are delicious in a salad of delicate greens.

Coriander (Cilantro): Coriander, sold often these days under its Mexican name, cilantro, has lovely tender, fringed leaves with a pungent, citrusy, slightly bitter flavor. A hearty annual, it was one of the original "bitter herbs" on the Seder plate at Passover celebrations. It's used often in Asian cooking; the Chinese call it Chinese parsley. Sparingly used, it is delicious garnishing avocados, tomatoes, and sweet Caribbean-style stews. The seeds, slightly sweet and more mild in flavor than the greens, are often used in cooking, usually ground first in a mortar.

Dill: A versatile, crowd-pleasing annual with tiny, feathery, fernlike leaves and a delicate aniselike flavor when used in small quantities, dill has a particular affinity for fish—and of course pickles. If overused, its flavor turns bitter and sharp, but used sparingly it enhances all kinds of seafood (it's especially great with shrimp: put some dill in the water when you boil them), potato salads, egg dishes, cottage cheese, cream cheese, soups, fresh vegetables (add dill to the cooking water when you boil green beans), and butter. Although the herb originated in the Mediterranean, the Romans disseminated it far and wide, and today it is particularly associated with Scandinavian cuisine.

Sweet Marjoram: Related to oregano, which is actually wild marjoram, sweet marjoram is a perennial usually grown as an annual, and has a sweeter, milder, more subtle flavor, enhanced by a hint of mint, than that of oregano. Its small, fragrant gray-green leaves and pretty pink late-summer flowers add the finishing touches to many dishes. It's nice in soups, clam dishes, chowders, broiled fish, eggplant dishes, chicken salad (combined with chives), and in chicken pot pies. The Germans use it to add distinctive flavor to sausages.

Mint: From the beginning of recorded history, and probably eons before that, mint, a bushy perennial, has been used both to stimulate the appetite and to calm digestion. There are a number of varieties, among them the mild spearmint and the peppery peppermint, the most popular and easiest to grow, and more exotic species, such as orange mint and pineapple mint. Bold and aggressive in the garden, mint, particularly peppermint and spearmint, spreads itself far and wide, trying to dominate—in my garden, at least—even the evergreens. Culinarily, too, it appears far and wide, used in almost every country in the world, and on menus in everything from hors d'oeuvres to desserts to after-dinner liqueurs. It adds its distinctive menthol essence to soups (sprinkle some in pea or lentil soup), salad dressings, roast or braised lamb, vegetables (wonderful with glazed carrots), chocolate desserts, and teas. And let us not forget how mint marries with bourbon in the incomparable mint julep, one of my favorite cocktails. As described in the writings of the Roman Pliny, Greeks even used mint to rub their wooden dining tables, both to treat the wood with the plant's essential oils and to stimulate the appetites of their guests with the plant's aroma.

Oregano (Wild Marjoram): A very hearty perennial that would be happy to take over your garden (vying with the mint) if you let it, oregano, cousin to sweet marjoram, is a wonderfully versatile herb, great in tomato sauces—and no less than essential in spaghetti sauce. And of course, no traditional pizza worth its salt, cheese, or tomato sauce should appear without a last-minute garnish of chopped oregano. It also enhances meatloaf and other beef dishes, eggplant, calf's liver (just a pinch), omelets, and tomato and lentil soups. Another herb disseminated by the Romans, oregano is a Mediterranean plant that originated in Syria and Palestine. For the Greeks, it was a symbol of happiness.

Parsley: This ubiquitous herb, a hearty biennial with a green, almost flinty flavor, is sadly still used more often as a garnish that's merely decorative, rather than as an ingredient per se. Originally from the Mediterranean, it comes in two varieties—flat-leaf, often called Italian parsley, which is more tender, with a more pronounced flavor, and curly or "moss-leaf," with a crisp texture and more subtle flavor. An essential herb in a bouquet garni and in groupings of *fines herbes,* parsley is extremely rich nutritionally, loaded with vitamin C, iron, and calcium. It is also full of chlorophyll (great for freshening breath). Its uses are myriad, in soups and stews, mixed with cottage cheese, combined with butter for steamed or baked potatoes, sprinkled on sliced tomatoes after drizzling with a tangy vinaigrette. It is even lovely all by itself as a side dish, gently steamed then tossed with a bit of salt and melted butter.

Rosemary: An aromatic, hearty perennial from the Mediterranean, with long, needlelike leaves and small, edible lavender-hued blossoms, rosemary can grow as big as a midrange evergreen in its native habitats. In Provence, old rosemary bushes can grow to more than seven feet tall. With its pungent, resinous flavor, rosemary, one of the true kitchen indispensables, subtly enhances many foods, especially roast lamb or chicken, potatoes, sauces, focaccia, stews, ragouts, marinades, stuffings, duck, teas (brew 1 teaspoon rosemary leaves per cup of water), and even in a recipe from the brilliant French chef Pierre Gagnaire, in a dessert soufflé with a single-malt scotch. In ancient days rosemary was believed to strengthen the memory, and has long been a symbol of remembrance, present at weddings, funerals, and memorial services. It is also said to dispel bad dreams; put some under your pillow for a blissful night of rest.

Sage: As its name suggests, shrubby, attractive sage, an evergreen perennial with soft, gray-green leaves, has long been associated with wisdom and sagacity. If you plant sage in your garden, it will grow luxuriantly and always offer you more than you'll know what to do with, since, as with many other herbs, just a little—a leaf or two—goes a very long way. Sage is a central ingredient in veal saltimbocca, and perks up stews, game, duck, goose, stewed tomatoes, and lima beans. Its distinctive tangy flavor, with subtle eucalyptus and cedar tones, works particularly well with pork, cutting the richness of the meat and enhancing digestibility. Most famously, sage is the star of all kinds of stuffing. In was an important component of medieval herb gardens, and, in ancient days, was often used in medicines. It's name in Latin—*Salvia*—means, in fact, "I am well."

Tarragon: With its long, slim, pungent leaves and licorice flavor, tarragon, a hardy perennial, enhances many foods in a wide variety of cuisines. Originating in western Asia and the Middle East, tarragon, although widely available these days, still has an exotic air about it. It is the essential ingredient in the cream sauce of a classic French chicken dish—chicken tarragon—as well as in one of the best of the flavored vinegars—tarragon vinegar. It also adds allure to fish broths, herb butters to top fish, seafood salad (especially great in a green mayonnaise served with chilled lobster), tomato soup and other tomato dishes, peas, and spinach. Tarragon is tasty in tartar sauce, sprinkled on baked or broiled fish just before serving, and if you like fish and chips the classic way (drizzled with vinegar), use tarragon vinegar instead of the classic malt vinegar for a real treat.

Thyme: There are at least sixty varieties of this pungent herb, with its tiny, dainty leaves and edible white flowers. Beyond the basic *Thymus vulgaris,* or common thyme, the most widely available are lemon thyme, orange thyme, and caraway thyme, each bearing the flavors of their names. An ancient herb originating in the Middle East, thyme, a hardy perennial, grows wild all over southern Europe, where it is frequently used in regional cooking. It adapts to almost any cuisine, and just a pinch makes almost anything more delicious, from soups (onion and vegetable), salads, fish and shellfish, meat loaves, roasts, cheese dishes, rice, shirred eggs, and—would you believe it—even chocolate and Bavarian cream. Used throughout the ages both medicinally and culinarily, it was also in days of yore routinely strewn about the floor, along with rosemary, sage, and other herbs, as a natural air freshener.

WHILE THE ABOVE THIRTEEN HERBS ARE THE MOST WIDELY AVAILABLE, and thus the most commonly used, the following group will add depth to your herbal palette. Apart from watercress most of these herbs unfortunately are not yet sold in regular grocery stores, so unless you live near an herb farm or a big urban green market, you'll have to grow them yourself.

Anise: While the seeds of anise, an annual, are often used in pastries and other baking, the feathery, deeply notched green leaves are much less present in cooking. They add a refreshing touch to fruit salads, beet salads, vegetable soups, and stews.

Borage: An alluring annual herb with luxuriant, fuzzy gray-green leaves, blue flowers, and a pronounced cucumber flavor, borage is tasty (using the flowers and smallest leaves) in salads, tomato soup, and iced teas, or floating in chilled wine-based beverages.

Caraway: This is a biennial herb used mainly for its seeds in cookies, cakes, breads, and roasts. But the pungent, feathery greens—finely chopped—are tasty too, adding intrigue to salads, soups, or steamed new potatoes.

Chervil: More delicate and feathery than parsley in look and flavor, chervil, an annual, is a sweet, aromatic herb with a hint of anise, delicious in salads; in sauces and stews; with eggs, fish, and chicken; and as a mixer with other delicate herbs such as chives and tarragon. It's very mild, so you can use a lot of it, pureed, for example, with other herbs, to make a rich green sauce for root vegetables. It is said to enhance the flavors of other herbs, which is why it is often used in *fines herbes* compositions.

Fennel: This is another anise-flavored herb, a hardy perennial with feathery tops resembling dill. Fennel leaves mix well with salad greens and potato salad, and add a delicious accent to fish—especially sea bass—and fish soups.

Lavender: One of the most delightfully fragrant herbs, with the most beautiful purple flowers, lavender, an annual or perennial depending upon the variety, is gaining popularity as a flavoring element, enhancing desserts, vinegars, even roast lamb. You can also make a subtly flavored lavender sugar by combining about ¼ cup fresh lavender blossoms with 1 cup sugar in a food processor. Keep sealed in a glass jar, and use for all kinds of baking (sprinkle on some sugar cookies) or sweetening teas in the teapot.

Lemon Balm: A little lemony, a little minty, this fragrant herb is nice for steeping with black or green teas—hot or iced—or infused on its own. Lemon balm, a perennial, has recently been enjoying increased popularity among sophisticated chefs. Use it in soups, roasts, fish, beets, and fruit salads.

Lemon Verbena: An ornamental, deciduous flowering shrub, lemon verbena is a striking addition to any herb garden. Its leaves and flowers make a soothing tea, as well as jams and jellies. Many chefs use it to add a bright, fresh lemony fragrance to stocks and fish sauces.

Lovage: A perennial herb that grows best near a freshwater source such as a gurgling brook, lovage, pungent and spicy with a distinct celerylike flavor, is delicious in hot restorative soups or with mussels, clams, and chicken dishes. Its tiny, yellow midsummer flowers are attractive in salads or floating in a chilled soup.

Nasturtium: Spicy and peppery nasturtiums, annuals with gorgeous orange and yellow edible blossoms, make a colorful flavored butter and are a wonderful addition to a summer salad, or garnishing grilled fish; always add just before serving.

Summer Savory: The tangy, subtle flavor of summer savory, an annual with tender leaves and dainty pinkish flowers, sparks the flavor of green beans, Brussels sprouts, cabbage, potato soups, and stews; use both leaves and flowers.

Winter Savory: A semi-evergreen perennial, winter savory, hardier and bushier than its summer cousin, works nicely with a variety of fish. Its glossy leaves are stronger and more intensely flavored than summer savory, so you need to use less of it to get a similar degree of flavor.

Sorrel: The slightly bitter, citrus-sour flavor of sorrel—a perennial with a large delicate leaf that resembles spinach, but that virtually melts when cooked, adds delicious contrast to a rich, creamy sauce. Terrific paired with salmon or other rich fish such as shad or pike, sorrel is also lovely in a soup with broth and potatoes or in an omelet.

Watercress: Not always recognized as an herb, watercress, an aquatic perennial that grows at the edges of brooks and streams, is a delicious, spicy, sharp-flavored salad green. It also makes a cool, crunchy base—dressed with oil, lemon juice, and soy sauce—for spicy tandoori-style chicken, or a flavorful soup, pureed with chicken broth and cream.

There are many more herbs left to discover, from angelica to yarrow—including the intriguingly named feverfew, rue, costmary, and valerian. These I leave for you to explore—and grow—on your own. A world of herbs awaits.

HARVESTING FRESH HERBS

If you have an herb garden, or simply an herb pot, the best time to gather a new batch is on a dry morning, after the dew has evaporated. Snip off the herbs with a small, sharp scissors, taking only as much as you need for your recipe.

HANDLING AND PREPARING FRESH HERBS

When preparing herbs for a recipe—chopping, mincing, or slicing in a julienne or chiffonade—use a small or medium very sharp knife that will slice through the herbs with one swipe. Slice in one direction, drawing the knife toward you. Avoid a back-and-forth sawing motion. Sharp little scissors, reserved for this purpose, are also an excellent tool for chopping or mincing herbs. If your herbs need to be pulverized or mashed, as in a pesto, a mortar and pestle do the job nicely.

STORING FRESH HERBS

Herbs should be stored in an airtight container, away from the light, ideally in cool surroundings. The top shelf of your fridge or the crisper drawer would be ideal. Store your herbs in sturdy plastic bags with a zipperlike seal, or in clean glass jars with airtight covers. A variety of green herbs can be stored like a little bouquet in a glass of water. Parsley, tarragon, chervil, and chives are among the herbs that stay perky in water. I also use this technique to revive sad, tired, limp herbs from the supermarket (sometimes that's all that's left). When I get home, I cut $1\frac{1}{2}$ to 2 inches from the bottom of the stems and place the tops in a glass of room-temperature water. Not all the sprigs revive, but enough do (after several hours) to give you ample plump, fresh-looking herbs for a recipe.

PRESERVING FRESH HERBS

Once herbs are preserved, they are, of course, no longer fresh. And with many fresh herbs now available in produce markets and supermarkets year round, it's no longer necessary to preserve many herbs for the cold, dark days of winter. But if you want to keep some prized herbs to use when the season is over, the best way to do this is to freeze them. There are several techniques for doing this:

• You can combine 1 packed cup herbs (leaves and sometimes tiny stems) and about $\frac{1}{2}$ cup water in a blender. Process until the herbs are finely chopped. Pour the resulting mixture into an ice-cube tray and freeze. When the cubes are frozen, place them in self-seal freezer bags, clearly marked. Over the next few months, drop a cube or two as needed into stews, ragouts, marinades—almost any time you need fresh herbs. You can also chop the herbs first, put them into ice-cube trays filling them almost to the top, then fill the rest of the tray with cold water. Freeze and proceed as above.

• You can blanch the fresh herbs by submerging them in boiling water for about 15 seconds. Drain, and pat dry. Chop them or leave them whole, then lay them in a single layer on a small tray, and place the tray in the freezer. When the herbs are frozen, place them in self-seal freezer bags, clearly labeled. They are ready to use at a moment's notice.

• If you have a true abundance of woody herbs, especially rosemary, and are looking for ways to take advantage of the bounty, use the sturdier rosemary sprigs as skewers to grill lamb. Strip off the leaves, then slide on the cubes of meat just as you would on a wooden skewer. The delicious, delicate fragrance and flavor of the rosemary permeates the meat as it grills. Save extra sprigs—or even stem bottoms—of rosemary and thyme in a basket by the fireplace, where they can gently dry. Use them on the grill, throwing two or three on the coals just before your meat or fish is done cooking, and let your dinner bask in the aromatic smoke for a minute or two before serving. Or throw a few sprigs on a gently burning fire on a winter's eve. The fragrance, detectable for only a sweet moment or two, is a delight, inspiring thoughts of summer barbecues to come.

appetizers

eggplant tian with sweet peppers and wild basil

A TIAN IS AN EARTHENWARE DISH USED FOR BAKING, but the term has been adapted by chefs to describe casserole-style dishes often baked in such a dish. In this simple, rustic version of a tian, from chef René Bérard, owner, with his wife, Danièle, of the charming Hostellerie Bérard in La Cadière-d'Azur in southern Provence, eggplant, onions, and sweet red peppers are layered with wild basil in a delicious, slow-cooked casserole in which the vegetables almost melt together. If you can't find wild basil, use common sweet basil. Even basil that has bolted—and is usually stronger flavored—will do, since the leaves nearly disintegrate as the dish bakes. You can serve the tian as a first course, as a simple, vegetarian main course with crusty French bread, or as a side dish with roasted meats.

SERVES 4

2 white onions
6 tablespoons olive oil
3 cloves garlic, peeled and crushed
3 medium eggplants
4 sweet red peppers
5 sprigs wild basil, stems removed
Salt
Freshly ground black pepper

Preheat the oven to 350° F. Peel and roughly chop the onions into 1-inch slices. Heat half the oil in a skillet and add the onions; cook until just tender, then add the garlic and sauté over medium heat until softened but not browned.

Meanwhile, peel the eggplants and cut them crosswise into ½-inch rounds. Cut the peppers lengthwise into quarters and remove the pith and seeds.

Spread the onions and garlic in the bottom of a 12-inch cast iron or earthenware roasting dish, and sprinkle with the basil. Arrange the eggplant and peppers in layers over the basil, ending with eggplant. Season with salt and pepper, and drizzle with the remaining oil.

Roast, occasionally pressing down on the vegetables with a spatula to make sure they are coated in oil and juices. Cook until most of the juices in the dish have evaporated and the vegetables are very soft, about 1½ hours. Serve hot from the roasting dish.

flaky chive and parmesan twists

THESE PUFF-PASTRY TWISTS ARE SIMPLE TO PREPARE, but make impressive-looking hors d'oeuvres to serve at impromptu gatherings. You'll just need to keep on hand a package of frozen puff pastry, some unsalted butter, a bit of Parmesan, and some chives or other fresh herbs. You could substitute sharp cheddar cheese for the Parmesan, or basil or tarragon for the chives; almost any variation of cheese and herbs that strikes you will work. These pastry twists are very adaptable.

MAKES ABOUT 2 DOZEN TWISTS

1 sheet ($\frac{1}{2}$ package, about $\frac{1}{2}$ pound) frozen puff pastry

4 tablespoons unsalted butter, softened

2 tablespoons minced chives

$\frac{1}{4}$ teaspoon salt

Freshly ground black pepper

$\frac{1}{4}$ tablespoon freshly squeezed lemon juice

$\frac{1}{2}$ cup freshly grated Parmigiano-Reggiano cheese

Half an hour before preparing, remove the sheet of puff pastry from the freezer, unwrap it, and set it aside on a plate to thaw. Do not try to unfold it before it thaws. Meanwhile, preheat the oven to 375° F.

In a small bowl, combine the butter, chives, salt, several generous turns of the pepper mill, and lemon juice, and mix with a small wooden spoon to combine; set aside.

When the dough is malleable, unfold it onto a lightly floured work surface. Using a sharp knife, cut the pastry dough into strips about 5 inches long and $\frac{3}{4}$ inch wide. Using a pastry brush or a small palette knife, lightly spread the butter mixture over the surface of each strip, leaving $\frac{1}{2}$ inch at the ends of each strip bare. Dust each strip with about 1 teaspoon of the cheese, then gently twist each strip into a spiral shape, giving each strip about 4 or 5 turns. Transfer to a nonstick baking sheet and gently press the ends onto the sheet to maintain the twisted form. Bake for 8 to 10 minutes, until the twists are puffy and golden brown. Arrange in a basket or on a serving tray, and serve immediately.

sage-marinated salmon
with red pepper salad

DELICATE AND FLAVORFUL, WITH JUST ENOUGH ZING from the peppers to enliven the palate, the sage-marinated salmon is a popular appetizer on the menu of the elegant and romantic Marbella Club Hotel on Spain's Costa del Sol.

SERVES 6

About 2 tablespoons olive oil for the ramekins
$1\frac{1}{4}$ pounds salt-cured salmon fillet, such as gravlax, thinly sliced
$2\frac{1}{4}$ pounds red bell peppers, roasted, peeled, seeded, and cut into thin strips
$\frac{1}{4}$ to $\frac{1}{3}$ cup extra-virgin olive oil
1 tablespoon minced sage leaves, plus 6 whole leaves
Coarse sea salt, or kosher salt
Freshly ground black pepper
1 to 2 tablespoons balsamic vinegar
1 large yellow bell pepper, roasted, peeled, and seeded

Brush the interior of six 4-inch ramekins or custard cups with olive oil. Divide the salmon among the ramekins, lining the sides and covering the bottoms. Reserve enough salmon to top the pepper salad in the filled ramekins.

Combine the red peppers with enough extra-virgin olive oil to coat. Add the minced sage and a pinch of salt and pepper, and toss to combine. Sprinkle with the balsamic vinegar, and toss again. Divide the pepper mixture among the ramekins, and cover with the remaining salmon, tucking in any overhanging ends.

Reserve any extra pepper slices to use as a garnish. Cover the ramekins with plastic wrap and refrigerate until very cold, about 3 hours.

To serve, remove the plastic wrap and unmold the salmon, reversing the ramekins onto individual plates. In a food processor, puree the yellow pepper with 1 to 2 tablespoons extra-virgin olive oil until smooth, season with salt and pepper to taste, then drizzle the mixture in a thin ribbon around the salmon. Garnish with a sage leaf and the reserved red peppers and serve.

chervil risotto
with white truffles

AT HIS DRAMATIC CONTEMPORARY RESTAURANT, Union Pacific, on Manhattan's West 22nd Street, Rocco DiSpirito, one of New York's most talented and innovative young chefs, serves this rich and luscious risotto in the fall, when the rare and delicate white truffle, from Italy's Alba region, comes into season. The aromatic truffles and herbs marry beautifully in the risotto, giving the dish an elegant earthy flavor that begins pleasing your senses the moment the plate is set down. The shaved white truffles are optional, since they are pricey and not always easy to find; the white truffle butter is available in many gourmet shops and by mail order from several sources listed in the back of this book.

SERVES 6 AS AN APPETIZER, 4 AS A MAIN COURSE

3 tablespoons unsalted butter
1 tablespoon olive oil
1 tablespoon chopped shallots
1 teaspoon chopped garlic
$1\frac{1}{2}$ cups Arborio (short-grain Italian) rice
1 bunch thyme, tied in a bundle
$\frac{1}{4}$ cup white wine
4 cups chicken stock
$\frac{2}{3}$ cup white truffle butter
$\frac{1}{4}$ cup chopped chervil
3 grams shaved white truffles (optional)

In a large saucepan over medium-low heat, combine 1 tablespoon of the plain butter with the oil and stir until the butter melts. Add the shallots and garlic and cook until the shallots are translucent but not browned, about 3 minutes. Add the rice and stir to coat with the butter. Add the thyme bundle and wine, stir, and cook until the mixture comes to a boil.

Meanwhile, in a separate pot, warm the stock. Add the stock to the rice 1 cup at a time, stirring occasionally, allowing the stock to be absorbed before adding the next cupful. Cook until the rice is tender but, as DiSpirito says, "toothsome." Remove and discard the thyme bundle. Stir in the truffle butter, the remaining 3 tablespoons plain butter, and the chervil. Remove from the heat, spoon into warmed serving bowls, and garnish, if you wish, with shaved white truffles. Serve immediately.

herb-marinated chèvre log

I MAKE THIS COUNTRY-STYLE APPETIZER IN AN OVAL, EARTHENWARE COVERED DISH about 10 inches long with 3-inch sides. Serve straight from the oval dish with slices of lightly toasted baguette.

SERVES 6 TO 8

One 6- to 8-inch chèvre log, ideally Montrachet
1 cup extra-virgin olive oil
2 small cloves crushed garlic
2 tablespoons chopped parsley
$\frac{1}{4}$ cup chopped scallions, white and pale green parts only
1 tablespoon thyme
1 tablespoon minced fresh marjoram
2 tablespoons finely julienned basil
Sea salt
Fresh coarsely ground black pepper

Place the chèvre log in a small ceramic oval dish with 3-inch sides. Pour the olive oil over and around the chèvre. Add the garlic, parsley, scallions, thyme, marjoram, basil, a generous pinch of salt, and several turns of the pepper mill, and gently stir into the oil.

Baste the log several times, then cover with plastic wrap or the dish cover and refrigerate. Marinate for 3 to 4 hours, basting the log every hour or so. Remove from the refrigerator 30 minutes before serving. Baste once more just before serving.

tapenade

THIS CLASSIC PROVENÇAL SPREAD is traditionally made with black olives from the region of Nice, or from those grown in the Provençal town of Nyons, combined with garlic, olive oil, anchovies, and sometimes lemon juice and basil. The tapenade is quite versatile, delicious spread on lightly grilled rounds of baguette, served as a vegetable dip, or used as a pasta sauce (with the addition of 3 more tablespoons of olive oil) tossed with hot ziti or penne or with a cold pasta salad.

MAKES ABOUT 1 CUP

1 cup pitted small, black Niçoise-style olives, or small Kalamata olives
1 clove garlic, crushed
2 anchovy fillets in oil, drained
1 teaspoon freshly squeezed lemon juice
2 teaspoons capers, drained
2 tablespoons extra-virgin olive oil
Freshly ground black pepper
4 basil leaves, coarsely chopped

In the bowl of a blender or small food processor, combine all the ingredients. Process until the mixture forms a smooth puree. Taste the mixture and adjust by adding more garlic, lemon juice, capers, basil, anchovies, pepper, or oil if needed. Transfer to a bowl, cover with plastic wrap, and refrigerate until ready to serve.

"mille-feuille" of zucchini and fresh herbs

A TRADITIONAL MILLE-FEUILLE IS A FRENCH PASTRY with multiple layers of flaky puff pastry separated by layers of fruit or pastry cream. But many chefs today use the term to describe a dish composed of multiple layers of a wide variety of ingredients, from apples to zucchini. In this recipe, created by Nito Carpita, the chef and proprietor, with her husband, David, of the Mas de Cornud in Provence, zucchini slices are layered with cheese and an herb cream, and then baked to create a delicious hot appetizer.

SERVES 4

4 large zucchini, ends trimmed
$\frac{1}{4}$ cup chopped herbs (mixture of rosemary, thyme, marjoram, parsley, stems removed)
5 ounces Gruyère cheese, shredded
1 teaspoon salt
2 tablespoons heavy cream
3 ounces freshly grated Parmigiano cheese

Cut each zucchini lengthwise into five $\frac{1}{4}$-inch slices. Bring a large pot of salted water to a boil and blanch the zucchini slices for about 8 minutes, until they are slightly softened but still hold their shape. Drain thoroughly, and cut each slice in half.

In a food processor combine the herbs and add half of the outer zucchini slices (discard the remaining outer slices or reserve for another use). Pulse until coarsely pureed. Then add the Gruyère, salt, and cream, and process until the texture is uniformly grainy. (The mixture can be prepared up to two days in advance and refrigerated; drain off excess liquid before using.) Transfer the mixture to a pastry bag.

Place 8 zucchini slices on a baking sheet lined with aluminum foil, and, using one-third of the herb mixture, pipe some onto each slice. Cover each of the eight portions of herb mixture with a second slice of zucchini. Press down gently, and, using another third of the herb mixture pipe some on top of each slice. Cover each portion with a third slice, and top with the remaining herb mixture. Sprinkle with the Parmigiano.

Preheat the broiler. Place the baking sheet about 4 inches from the flame, and broil until the tops are evenly browned, about 5 minutes. Use a thin spatula to carefully transfer the "mille-feuille" to individual serving plates. Serve immediately.

creamy herb and spinach vegetable dip

THIS IS ONE OF MY FAVORITE DIPS, fresh and tangy, perfect with cut vegetables such as carrots, broccoli, fennel, zucchini, cucumbers, and celery, as well as with a variety of chips. It's even better made a day ahead. For a festive presentation, serve the dip in a hollowed-out red cabbage "bowl" surrounded by the cut vegetables.

MAKES ABOUT 4 CUPS

1 cup mayonnaise

1 cup sour cream

$\frac{1}{2}$ cup chives or scallions, chopped

$\frac{1}{2}$ cup chopped parsley

$\frac{1}{4}$ cup chopped dill

1 small chopped shallot

$\frac{1}{2}$ small clove garlic, minced

1 teaspoon salt

$\frac{1}{2}$ teaspoon celery seed

$\frac{1}{2}$ teaspoon freshly squeezed lemon juice

2 cups cooked spinach, drained and squeezed of excess water

In the bowl of a food processor, combine the mayonnaise, sour cream, chives, parsley, dill, shallot, garlic, salt, celery seed, and lemon juice. Process for several seconds until blended. Add the spinach and process until thoroughly blended. Adjust the seasoning, and add a little more sour cream if you find the dip too thick. Transfer to a bowl, cover tightly with plastic wrap, and refrigerate for several hours, or even overnight, before serving.

mediterranean stuffed tomatoes
with herbed tuna and rice

INTENSELY FLAVORFUL AND AROMATIC, these stuffed tomatoes are an adaptation of a dish I had on the French Riviera, in a café overlooking the port in Villefranche-sur-Mer. They make a delicious cold appetizer, or a distinctive addition to a buffet table.

SERVES 6

6 large, firm, ripe tomatoes

$3/4$ teaspoon salt

2 tablespoons freshly squeezed lemon juice

$3/4$ cup extra-virgin olive oil

1 cup cooked rice, cold

1 large pearl onion, thinly sliced

5 large shallots, thinly sliced

1 large clove garlic, minced

1 teaspoon thyme

$1/2$ teaspoon freshly ground black pepper

Three 6-ounce cans light albacore tuna packed in oil, drained and flaked

$3/4$ cup chopped chives

$3/4$ cup chopped cilantro

$1/3$ cup chopped basil

6 small sprigs basil (optional)

Using a sharp knife, slice off the top third of the tomatoes, and set aside. Scoop out the seeds from the tomatoes, sprinkle about $1/4$ teaspoon salt into the cavities and turn them upside down to drain. Set aside.

In a medium bowl, combine the lemon juice with 2 tablespoons of the oil and whisk to emulsify. Add the rice and toss to coat thoroughly with the dressing; set aside.

In a large skillet, heat 3 tablespoons of the oil over medium heat. Add the onion, shallots, garlic, thyme, the remaining $1/2$ teaspoon salt and pepper, and stir to combine. Lower the heat to medium-low and cook until the onion and shallots become translucent, about 4 minutes. Remove from the heat and set aside to cool.

In the bowl of an electric mixer, combine the tuna, onion mixture, chives, cilantro, and the chopped basil, and mix on medium-low speed, slowly drizzling the remaining oil into the mixture, and scraping down the sides, until thoroughly blended. Remove the bowl from the mixer, add the rice mixture, and stir with a wooden spoon until combined. Adjust the seasoning.

Set the tomatoes right side up on a platter. Using a tablespoon, stuff each tomato, so that the stuffing is generously mounded above the tomato. Place the tomato caps at a slight angle on top of the stuffing. Garnish with sprigs of basil, if you wish, cover with plastic wrap, and refrigerate until ready to serve. Serve slightly chilled, but not cold.

gelée of aromatic herbs
with red grapes

PIERRE GAGNAIRE, CHEF OF HIS SELF-NAMED three-star restaurant on the rue Balzac in Paris, is one of the world's most brilliant and creative chefs. In the highly competitive world of gastronomy, his work is unique. This recipe is a case in point. The base is an exquisitely pure, almost ethereal, clear jellied broth, with a pale celadon tint and an intense, aromatic herb flavor. Peeled red grapes coated with fine bread crumbs rest on top of this jelly—a juxtaposition as unusual as it is magical. Chef Gagnaire also suggests the jellied herb broth as a base for presenting steamed, deveined shrimp, sliced in half lengthwise.

SERVES 4

1 liter of Evian, or other flat mineral water
1/2 medium white onion, minced
1/2 cup chopped and mixed aromatic herbs,
   ideally at least 4 from among:
     tarragon, parsley, chives, cilantro, chervil,
     lovage, celery leaves
Three 1/4-inch-thick round slices lemon

Three 1/4-inch-thick round slices lime
1/4 teaspoon salt
1/2 teaspoon coarsely ground black pepper
Two 1/4-ounce packets gelatin
20 seedless red grapes
1/2 cup fine bread crumbs

In a large saucepan, combine the mineral water with the onion and bring to a boil over high heat. Lower the heat to medium and cook at a gentle boil for 5 minutes. Remove from the heat, stir in the herbs, lemon, lime, salt, and pepper, and set aside. Sprinkle the gelatin over 1/3 cup cold water and stir to dissolve. Pour into the herb broth, and stir to combine thoroughly; make sure that the gelatin is completely dissolved. Pour through a fine-mesh sieve and set aside to cool. When the mixture is cool, but not set, ladle into 4 individual soup bowls, then refrigerate for several hours, until firmly set.

Meanwhile, prepare the grapes. Bring a pot of water to a boil over high heat. Add the grapes and cook for 1 minute. Using a slotted spoon, remove the grapes to a small bowl. When the grapes are cool enough to handle, carefully peel off the skins, using the tip of a paring knife and your fingers. Place the bread crumbs in a small bowl, then roll each grape in the bread crumbs to cover; place on a small plate. Lightly cover the plate with plastic wrap and refrigerate until ready to serve.

Place 5 grapes in a circle on top of each serving of jellied broth and serve immediately.

soups

broccoli soup
with goat cheese and basil

THIS RICHLY FLAVORED, BRIGHT GREEN SOUP was created by Sue Chapman, chef of the serene California spa The Lodge at Skylonda. The basil adds depth of flavor to the soup's broccoli and spinach base, further enhanced by a bit of sherry.

SERVES 6

2 teaspoons olive oil

1 cup chopped onion

2 teaspoons minced garlic

1 tablespoon flour

$\frac{1}{4}$ cup sweet sherry

2 cups chicken stock

4 cups broccoli florets

1 cup fresh spinach, firmly packed

2 tablespoons chopped basil

4 ounces fresh goat cheese

1 cup 2% milk

Salt

White pepper

In a soup pot, heat the oil over medium heat. Add the onion and garlic and sauté until soft but not brown, about 2 minutes. Dust the pan with the flour, then add the sherry and stir to combine, scraping up any browned bits on the bottom of the pan. Add the stock and cook until the mixture reaches a slow simmer. Add $3\frac{1}{2}$ cups of the broccoli and cook until the broccoli is just tender but still retains its bright green color, about 3 minutes. Transfer the mixture to the bowl of a food processor. Add the spinach, basil, and half of the goat cheese, and puree. Return the mixture to the pot, then add the milk and stir to combine. Season with salt and pepper to taste. Ladle into warmed soup bowls, garnish with the remaining broccoli and goat cheese, and serve.

butternut squash–green apple soup

THIS IS A LIGHT AND VERY PRETTY SOUP from chef Todd Weisz at the Turnberry Isle Resort and Club in Aventura, Florida. It would be a perfect first course at a Thanksgiving dinner, or any dinner, preceding a copious and rich main course. The bouquet garni enhances the delicate flavor of the squash and apples, while the scallions add their mild, oniony flavor as well as texture and color contrast. The optional crème fraîche's creamy, tangy flavor contributes depth and richness.

SERVES 6

3 cups peeled, seeded, and chopped butternut squash
$1\frac{1}{4}$ cups peeled, cored, and diced green apples, such as Granny Smith
1 large onion, diced
$2\frac{1}{2}$ cups chicken stock
$\frac{1}{2}$ teaspoon salt
Freshly ground white pepper
1 bouquet garni with 2 sprigs thyme, 1 sprig rosemary, 1 clove garlic, and 1 bay leaf
2 tablespoons crème fraîche (optional)
3 scallions, pale green parts only, thinly sliced

In a medium saucepan, combine the squash, apple, onion, stock, salt, a generous pinch of white pepper, and the bouquet garni. Bring the mixture to a boil, cover, and lower the heat to maintain a simmer. Cook until the ingredients are very tender, 20 to 30 minutes.

Remove the bouquet garni, pour the mixture into a food processor or blender, and puree until smooth. Ladle the soup into warmed serving bowls. Swirl a teaspoon-size dollop of crème fraîche, if using, in the center of each bowl. Garnish with the scallions, and serve.

la cadière melon soup with mint

SUMMERTIME IN PROVENCE IS A LONG, SUNNY, HOT SEASON that yields a bounty of beautiful, fragrant fruits and vegetables. The sweet, heavy, orange-fleshed melons, particularly those from the region of Cavaillon, are among the region's most eagerly awaited crops. These ambrosial melons are best served very simply, perhaps with a bit of port wine in the center, or in elemental recipes where the character and flavor of the melon shines through. In this recipe from Provençal chef René Bérard, proprietor of the Hostellerie Bérard in La Cadière-d'Azur, a village nestled in the hills above the Mediterranean, the melon is macerated overnight in orange juice, sherry, crème fraîche, and mint. The result is an aromatic, refreshing dish—not particularly soupy, but rather melon in a creamy sauce—appropriate either at the start of a meal or at the end, as sweet and welcoming as a breeze at the end of a Provençal summer day.

SERVES 4 TO 6

1 large, ripe orange-flesh melon, flesh cut into bite-size pieces
¼ cup fresh orange juice
¼ cup dry sherry
½ cup plus 2 tablespoons crème fraîche
1 bunch mint
1 lemon, cut into paper-thin rounds

In a large glass bowl, combine the melon, orange juice, sherry, and crème fraîche. Stir gently to combine. Stir in 5 sprigs of mint, then cover the bowl with plastic wrap and refrigerate overnight.

Remove and discard the mint, stir, then spoon the melon mixture into chilled serving bowls. Garnish each serving with a lemon round and a sprig of mint. Serve immediately.

cream of watercress soup
with sevruga caviar

THIS ELEGANT SOUP WAS THE FIRST course of a memorable meal I had at Le Cinq, at the Four Seasons Hotel George V in Paris. Celebrated chef Philippe Legendre, formerly of Paris's acclaimed Taillevent restaurant, created this soup to combine the "essence of two seas," as he puts it—watercress from the fresh-water streams, caviar from the ocean. If sevruga caviar is a little rich for your budget, substitute golden lumpfish caviar, available in many supermarkets and gourmet shops.

SERVES 6

2 tablespoons unsalted butter

1 small onion, finely chopped

1 leek, white and pale green parts only, trimmed and finely chopped

3 cups chicken stock

3 cups light cream

1 tablespoon plus $\frac{1}{2}$ teaspoon salt

3 bunches watercress, leaves and tiny stems only

$\frac{1}{2}$ cup crème fraîche

2 ounces sevruga or lumpfish caviar

In a heavy-bottomed casserole, melt the butter over medium heat. Add the onion and leek and cook, stirring frequently, until they become soft and slightly translucent, about 3 minutes. Add the stock, raise the heat slightly, and bring to a boil. Lower the heat to medium-low and simmer for 10 minutes. Add the light cream and cook for 10 minutes longer, keeping the mixture at a simmer; do not let it boil. Remove from the heat, stir in $\frac{1}{2}$ teaspoon of the salt, cover, and set aside.

Bring a large saucepan of water to a boil over high heat. Add the remaining tablespoon of salt, then add the watercress, lower the heat to medium-high, and cook for 2 minutes. Meanwhile, prepare an ice water bath for the watercress. Drain the watercress then plunge it immediately into the ice water bath to stop the cooking. When the watercress is cold, drain and set aside.

Strain the stock mixture into a bowl through a fine chinois or a very fine sieve lined with rinsed and squeezed cheesecloth. Stir in the watercress. Working in batches, transfer the mixture to a blender or the bowl of a food processor. Process until the mixture is completely blended, about 30 seconds per batch. Adjust the seasoning, then transfer to a covered container and set aside, or chill until ready to serve. (You can prepare the recipe several hours ahead up to this point.) In a mixing bowl, beat the crème fraîche with a whisk until it forms soft peaks. Set aside, or chill until ready to serve.

To serve, heat the soup in a large saucepan over medium heat, until very hot but not boiling. Ladle into small warmed soup bowls. Spoon a dollop of whipped crème fraîche into the center of each bowl. Carefully spoon a rounded teaspoonful of caviar onto each mound of crème fraîche; the crème fraîche and caviar should almost float in the center of the bowl. Serve immediately.

lovage soup

THIS LOVELY, FLAVORFUL SOUP IS ONE OF THE TREASURED RECIPES of the New York Unit of the Herb Society of America, contributed by member Betsey Sluder. The soup, resembling a warm vichyssoise, is served every year at their annual Herb Fair at the John Jay Homestead in Katonah, New York. The Herb Society of America was founded in 1933, originally to promote and study American-grown herbs, and the New York Unit, dedicated to the growth and study of local herbs, was formed shortly thereafter, in 1938. The unit's activities today are multifaceted: the society organizes herb garden tours and herb symposiums, supports public gardens and environmental projects, and has created its own cookbook, *For Use and for Delight: A Herbal Sampler,* one of my personal favorites.

SERVES 6 TO 8

2 tablespoons unsalted butter

2 leeks, white part only, minced

2 white onions, chopped

4 eastern baking potatoes, such as Maine russets, peeled and thinly sliced

3 cups chicken stock

$\frac{1}{2}$ teaspoon salt

1 cup shredded lovage leaves

3 cups half-and-half

In a heavy saucepan, melt 1 tablespoon of the butter over medium heat. Stir in the leeks and onion and cook until they are soft and slightly translucent, but not browned, about 4 minutes. Add the potatoes, stock, and salt, and cook, stirring occasionally, until the potatoes are very soft, about 40 minutes.

Meanwhile, melt the remaining 1 tablespoon butter in a small skillet over medium heat, stir in the lovage, cover, lower the heat to medium-low, and cook until the lovage is softened, about 3 minutes. Remove from the heat and set aside.

Press the potato mixture through a fine sieve or a potato ricer into a large saucepan (or process in a blender or food processor, then transfer to a saucepan). Add the lovage and the half-and-half, stir to combine, then place over medium heat until very hot, but not boiling. Serve immediately in warmed soup bowls.

chilled basque white bean soup
with prosciutto

HÉLÈNE DARROZE IS A YOUNG chef from southwest France whose savory, seductive cuisine, inspired by a family tradition of gastronomy that stretches back to the late 1800s, took Paris by storm when she opened her intimate Left Bank restaurant in 1999. The first woman in a four-generation line of distinguished chefs from Villeneuve-de-Marsan, a town in the Landes region between Bordeaux and Biarritz, Darroze apprenticed with world-famous chef Alain Ducasse at his restaurant Le Louis XV in Monaco before taking over the family restaurant in Villeneuve-de-Marsan. Then, fulfilling her dream, she moved to Paris to open a restaurant bearing her name. Her cuisine is generous and innovative, featuring elaborate, slow-cooked dishes of great quality and finesse—dishes like tomatoes stuffed with foie gras and duck confit, brioche French toast with plum marmalade, and this distinctly southwestern recipe, chilled Basque white bean soup, savory with thyme, bay leaf, parsley, and prosciutto.

SERVES 6 TO 8

8 tablespoons olive oil

1 large carrot, finely diced

1 large onion, finely diced

2 ounces thick-cut prosciutto, finely diced

1 pound dried white beans, such as navy or
  Great Northern, soaked overnight in water
  to cover, and drained

5 cups chicken stock

1 sprig fresh rosemary

1 bouquet garni (small sachet of bay leaf,
  thyme sprig, parsley sprig)

Salt

Freshly ground white pepper

2 tablespoons chopped parsley

6 to 8 parsley sprigs, for garnish

2 ounces prosciutto, sliced paper thin, half
  minced, half cut into 2-inch squares, for garnish

1 cup light cream

3 tablespoons sherry vinegar

In a large casserole or Dutch oven, heat 3 tablespoons of the oil over medium heat. Add the carrot, onion, and diced, thick-cut prosciutto, and stir to combine. Cook until the prosciutto turns lightly browned, and the onions and carrots soften, about 4 minutes. Add the beans, stock, rosemary, and bouquet garni, and stir to combine. Cover, lower the heat to medium-low, and cook for about 1 hour, until the beans are tender. Add a pinch of salt and pepper to taste, then remove the rosemary and bouquet garni and discard. With a slotted spoon, transfer ½ cup of the beans to a small container, cover with plastic wrap, and reserve in the refrigerator. Transfer the rest of the bean mixture and broth to the bowl of a food processor or a blender and puree until smooth and velvety, about 45 seconds. Transfer to a bowl and cover with plastic wrap, or to a plastic storage container with a cover, and refrigerate until thoroughly chilled, about 2 hours. (You can make the soup up to this point a day ahead.)

Just before serving, warm up the ½ cup of reserved beans in the microwave or in a small saucepan, then mash them lightly and set aside. In a small skillet over medium heat, heat 2 tablespoons of the oil. Add the chopped parsley and the minced, thin-sliced prosciutto, stir to combine, and cook until the parsley and prosciutto are warmed through, about 2 minutes. Transfer to a plate covered with paper towels. In a small bowl, combine the mashed beans with the parsley-prosciutto mixture and the remaining 3 tablespoons of the oil, and stir briskly to blend.

Add the cream and the vinegar to the bean puree and whisk to blend. Adjust the seasoning to taste, then ladle into soup bowls. Place a spoonful of the mashed-bean mixture in the center of each bowl, then garnish the surface of each serving with a square of prosciutto and a parsley sprig next to the mashed bean mixture; serve immediately.

accompaniments

fresh mint sauce

FRESHLY MADE MINT SAUCE, to serve with hot or cold lamb, has a lighter and more truly minty flavor than the bottled variety. Make it several hours ahead of serving or even the day before.

MAKES ABOUT 1 CUP

$^2/_3$ cup white wine vinegar
$^3/_4$ cup mint leaves, minced
2 tablespoons brown sugar
$^1/_2$ teaspoon salt
Freshly ground white or black pepper

In a small ceramic or glass bowl, combine all the ingredients with 3 tablespoons cold water. Whisk vigorously until the sugar and salt are dissolved. Cover with plastic wrap and refrigerate for at least several hours, or overnight, to allow the flavors to develop. Whisk again just before serving.

herbed rémoulade sauce

THIS IS A VARIATION OF THE TRADITIONAL FRENCH RÉMOULADE, a cold, mayonnaise-based sauce with Dijon mustard. It is often used plain, mixed with shredded celery root, or dressed up with gherkins, capers, and herbs to serve with cold fish, shellfish, or meat.

MAKES ABOUT 1 ½ CUPS

1 tablespoon freshly squeezed lemon juice

¼ teaspoon salt

¼ teaspoon freshly ground white or black pepper

1 cup mayonnaise

2 tablespoons Dijon mustard

3 baby gherkins, finely diced

1 tablespoon minced parsley

1 tablespoon minced tarragon

1 tablespoon minced chives

1 tablespoon thoroughly drained capers, minced

In a glass or ceramic bowl, combine the lemon juice, salt, and pepper and whisk until the salt dissolves. Add the mayonnaise and mustard and whisk. Add all the remaining ingredients and whisk to combine. Cover with plastic wrap and refrigerate for several hours before serving.

charred pineapple relish
with thai basil and orange mint

AT THE FEDERALIST, THE RESTAURANT WITHIN FIFTEEN BEACON, a chic boutique hotel atop Boston's Beacon Hill, executive chef Eric Brennan creates an innovative and dazzling menu that draws Bostonians from every corner of the city. His charred pineapple relish with Thai basil and orange mint is an exotic condiment that he serves with grilled seafood, poultry, or pork. If you can't find Thai basil, use the common sweet basil; if orange mint is not available, use the smallest leaves of peppermint along with 1 tablespoon orange juice.

MAKES 5 CUPS

1 pineapple

1 red onion, peeled

2 sweet peppers (mixture of red, yellow, or green), stems and seeds removed

1 cup rice wine vinegar

$\frac{1}{4}$ cup sugar

1 tablespoon finely minced Thai red chilies

A few dashes of Thai fish sauce (*nam pla*)

Salt

Freshly ground black pepper

1 bunch Thai basil, stems removed

1 bunch orange mint, stems removed

Prepare a charcoal fire or preheat the broiler or a stovetop grill pan.

Cut the pineapple into quarters lengthwise, slice off the rind and the core, and use a paring knife to cut out the "eyes." Grill or broil the pineapple quarters until charred and browned on all sides, turning occasionally, about 15 minutes total. Set aside to cool.

Dice the onion, sweet peppers, and pineapple.

In a small saucepan bring the vinegar and sugar to a boil; add the onion and cook for 3 minutes, until soft. In a mixing bowl combine the pineapple, sweet peppers, chilies, and fish sauce, and pour the vinegar mixture over. Season to taste with salt and pepper and let cool to room temperature.

Chop the herbs; add to the relish and stir to combine. Serve at room temperature.

garlic butter

I KEEP THIS BUTTER ON HAND, in the fridge or freezer, for making garlic bread on the spur of the moment. (I've also used this butter to brighten a piece of grilled fish or a small steak—a round teaspoonful placed on top of each serving.) The parsley, lemon juice, and garlic are constants, to which I add a teaspoon or so of whatever other fresh herbs I happen to have—thyme, oregano, marjoram, chervil. Slice crusty Italian bread lengthwise, spread it generously with garlic butter, then place under the broiler and cook until the tops of the bread are browned and bubbly, about 2 minutes.

MAKES ABOUT $3/4$ CUP

$1/2$ cup salted butter, softened
1 tablespoon chopped garlic
3 tablespoons chopped parsley
1 teaspoon of one of the following chopped herbs: thyme, oregano, marjoram, chervil
$1/2$ teaspoon freshly squeezed lemon juice
$1/2$ teaspoon freshly ground black pepper

In a mixing bowl, combine all the ingredients, then mix with a wire whisk until thoroughly blended. Transfer the butter to a ceramic butter bell or a ramekin or other small bowl, cover with plastic wrap, and refrigerate; or roll butter mixture into a log shape, wrap in plastic wrap and freeze until ready to use.

basil and eggplant pesto

THIS DELICIOUS VARIATION ON A TRADITIONAL PESTO, with roasted eggplant, was devised by Denis Jaricot, Executive Chef of the CuisinArt Resort on Anguilla. One of the resort's most unusual amenities is its hydroponic garden, where delicate herbs and vegetables grow in nutrient-spiked water throughout the year. Chef Jaricot uses ingredients harvested daily from the garden in most of his dishes.

SERVES 4

1 large eggplant (about 1½ pounds), halved lengthwise

½ cup plus 2 tablespoons extra-virgin olive oil

Coarse salt

1 clove garlic, finely chopped

3 tablespoons pine nuts

2 tightly packed cups basil

½ cup freshly grated Parmigiano-Reggiano cheese

½ cup freshly grated Pecorino cheese

Preheat the oven to 400° F. Lightly score the cut surfaces of the eggplant halves, brush with 2 tablespoons of the oil, and sprinkle generously with salt. Place in a baking pan face up and bake until very soft and tender, 30 to 45 minutes. Scoop out the roasted eggplant flesh and set aside; discard the peel.

In the bowl of a food processor or a blender, combine the garlic, pine nuts, and a pinch of salt. Process or blend to make a smooth paste. Add the basil leaves a few at a time, and continue to process. Drizzle in the remaining ½ cup oil, and gradually add the cheeses, continuing to process, until the oil, cheese, and basil are incorporated and no large pieces of basil are visible. Add the eggplant and process to a smooth puree. Store covered in the refrigerator.

To serve with pasta, dilute the pesto with 1 to 2 tablespoons of pasta cooking water (unless the pasta remains a little wet, in which case no extra water is necessary), and toss.

provençal olive-rosemary butter

AS AN HORS D'OEUVRE SPREAD, or to serve at the table with fresh baguettes or sourdough rolls, this intensely flavorful butter from chef Jean-François Meteigner of La Cachette in Los Angeles is always a hit. The rosemary, garlic, and black olives, each redolent of Provence, form a complementary trio. The butter will keep in the refrigerator for over a week, or in the freezer sealed in plastic wrap, for at least a month.

MAKES ABOUT ²/₃ CUP

½ cup unsalted butter, softened
2 tablespoons pitted and finely chopped black olives
1½ teaspoons chopped rosemary
1 teaspoon chopped garlic
1 teaspoon freshly ground black pepper

In a small skillet over medium heat, melt 1 tablespoon of the butter. Add the rosemary and sauté for 10 seconds, stirring constantly, just to release some of the rosemary flavor. Set aside in the pan to cool. Combine the remaining butter with the olives, garlic, pepper, and the cooled sautéed rosemary, then mix with a wire whisk until thoroughly combined.

Fill a ceramic butter bell or a ramekin with the butter, cover with plastic wrap, and refrigerate until chilled, about 2 hours.

vermouth crème fraîche
seafood sauce with dill and chervil

FROM ERIC BRENNAN, CHEF OF THE STYLISH Federalist Restaurant in Boston, a town that takes its seafood seriously, comes this rich, easy, and versatile sauce perfect for poaching small pieces of fish or shellfish. Try it with salmon fillets cut into strips, shelled shrimp, shucked scallops, or oysters.

SERVES 4 AS AN APPETIZER, 2 AS A MAIN COURSE

$\frac{1}{2}$ cup dry white vermouth
2 tablespoons minced shallots
1 cup crème fraîche
$\frac{1}{2}$ cup fish stock or chicken stock
Salt
Freshly ground black pepper
1 pound salmon fillets or other seafood
1 tablespoon chopped dill
Small bunch chervil, leaves only

In a medium stainless steel or enameled saucepan, combine the vermouth and shallots, set over medium heat, and cook, stirring occasionally, until the vermouth is reduced by half, about 5 minutes. Add the crème fraîche and stir to blend. Bring to a simmer, then add the stock and a pinch of salt and pepper, and cook until the mixture just comes to a boil. Add the seafood, cover the pot, and cook until the seafood is just cooked through, usually 3 to 7 minutes. Add the dill and chervil and stir to combine; adjust the seasoning to taste. Serve with pasta.

sorrel sauce

IN THIS CLASSIC FRENCH SAUCE, almost decadent in our health-conscious age, the tang from the crème fraîche and the tartness of the sorrel contrast winningly with the velvety richness of the butter, egg, and cream base. This sauce is most delicious served on top of a simple poached salmon fillet, where the tart sauce and the sweet fish create a perfect yin and yang. Pair the fish with tiny steamed new potatoes garnished with butter and parsley.

SERVES 4 TO 6

6 tablespoons unsalted butter
1 pound sorrel, tough stems removed, sliced into thin julienne
1 sprig thyme
1 sprig sage
1 sprig parsley
$\frac{1}{4}$ teaspoon salt
Freshly ground black pepper
4 egg yolks
$1\frac{1}{3}$ cup crème fraîche

In a large skillet, melt the butter over medium heat. Add the sorrel, thyme, sage, and parsley, and stir to coat with butter. Cover the pan and cook, stirring occasionally, until the sorrel is completely wilted and tender, about 10 minutes. Uncover, add the salt and several turns of the pepper mill, and continue to cook, stirring often, until all excess liquid evaporates, about 2 minutes. Remove from the heat. Pick out and discard the thyme, sage, and parsley sprigs. Press the sorrel mixture through a fine strainer or a food mill, or puree in a blender. Set aside.

In a medium mixing bowl, combine the egg yolks and the crème fraîche and beat until blended and frothy. Add the pureed sorrel and stir to combine. Pour the mixture into a saucepan, set over medium-low heat, and warm, stirring constantly, until the mixture thickens. Adjust the seasoning, then transfer the mixture to a warmed sauceboat and serve immediately.

A few pinches of fresh herbs stirred in at the last minute add distinction to a wide variety of gravies and sauces. One of the easiest ways to do this is to use a tablespoon or two of an herb butter that you have on hand, either in the freezer or the refrigerator. If you frequently make gravies or sauces after preparing a roast or a fish, it would make sense to have several herb butters on hand for this purpose. One stick of softened unsalted butter combined with 4 tablespoons of a chopped fresh herb, plus a dash of lemon juice and a pinch of salt and pepper does the trick: use this method with rosemary, sage, winter savory, or thyme for meats; dill, basil, or chives for fish; tarragon or rosemary for chicken. For a savory butter to finish a gravy for game or rich red meats, combine the stick of butter with 1 tablespoon oregano, 1 tablespoon winter savory, 1 teaspoon ground juniper berries, a few drops of lemon juice, and a pinch of salt and pepper. Store the butters, covered in plastic wrap, in ramekins or butter bells for the refrigerator, or rolled into logs and wrapped in freezer wrap for the freezer. Following are a few other suggestions for finishing sauces or gravies with herbs if you don't have herb butters on hand.

For a flavorful HOLLANDAISE SAUCE, toss in 1 or 2 tablespoons chopped tarragon just after the sauce has thickened. A tarragon hollandaise is lovely over baked fish such as striped bass or halibut, and makes an interesting change of pace on eggs Benedict.

For a delicious, savory gravy for a ROAST LEG OF LAMB, add 2 tablespoons butter, 1 tablespoon chopped sage, $\frac{1}{2}$ teaspoon pulverized rosemary, and 1 teaspoon anchovy paste to the deglazed pan juices. (The flavor of anchovy is a surprisingly compatible taste with lamb; I occasionally add bits of anchovy wherever I press in a clove of garlic when preparing a leg of lamb for roasting, a technique I learned in Provence.)

For a tasty sauce for POACHED FISH, add the following to the court-bouillon, white wine, or fish stock in which you've poached your fish: 1 tablespoon minced dill or marjoram, 1 tablespoon minced parsley, $\frac{1}{2}$ teaspoon freshly squeezed lemon juice, a pinch of salt and freshly ground black pepper. To this you could also add 2 tablespoons unsalted butter and stir to blend; or 4 tablespoons crème fraîche; or 1 beaten egg yolk, whisked into the sauce after it's removed from the heat.

Be creative when finishing your sauces and gravies, and don't be afraid to experiment. Just remember that a little goes a long way, as far as herbs are concerned. Sauces are a delicate balance of flavors, and herbs should be just one note of the composition.

salads and
dressings

tarragon vinaigrette
à la san régis

A GLOWING GEM OF A SMALL PARIS HOTEL, the exclusive San Régis, on the rue Jean Goujon just off the Champs-Elysées, has an intimate dining room that feels more like a private club than a public restaurant. Here chef Jean-Marc Lappel turns out light, imaginative meals, several using creative vinaigrettes, such as this one. The delicate anise flavor from the tarragon, combined with the three oils and the balsamic vinegar, makes this a perfect dressing for a salad of delicate greens, for steamed green vegetables such as asparagus, or for a grilled fillet of fish.

SERVES 6

2 tablespoons balsamic vinegar
¼ teaspoon salt
⅛ teaspoon freshly ground black pepper
2 small shallots, minced
1 teaspoon finely chopped sage
2 tablespoons finely chopped tarragon
4 tablespoons extra-virgin olive oil
2 tablespoons peanut oil
2 tablespoons hazelnut oil

In a small bowl, combine the vinegar, salt, and pepper, and whisk until the salt dissolves. Add the shallots and herbs and stir to combine. Add the three oils and whisk to emulsify. Serve immediately.

minted cider vinaigrette

THIS IS ANOTHER IMAGINATIVE VINAIGRETTE from Jean-Marc Lappel, chef of the Hotel San Régis in Paris. Flecked with mint and spiced with just a soupçon of cinnamon and Tabasco, it was created as a light, piquant dressing for warm grilled sea scallops. Chef Lappel also recommends it as a dressing for a salad of mixed citrus fruits, such as orange, pink grapefruit, and tangerine sections.

SERVES 6

1 tablespoon cider vinegar
3 tablespoons finely julienned mint
$\frac{1}{2}$ cup grapeseed oil
$\frac{1}{4}$ teaspoon salt
Small pinch of cinnamon
3 drops Tabasco

In a small bowl, combine the vinegar with the mint. Add the oil and whisk to blend. Add the salt, cinnamon, and the Tabasco and whisk to emulsify. Serve immediately.

greek country salad

THIS SALAD IS AN ADAPTATION OF A TRADITIONAL salad known as *horiatiki*, served in almost every *taverna* and on many family tables in small villages throughout Greece. The common elements in the salads are ripe summer tomatoes, feta cheese, and thinly sliced red onions. To this foundation you can add one or more of the following ingredients: Kalamata olives, fresh oregano, salted sardines, scallions, hard-boiled eggs, parsley, and cucumbers. Some salads are dressed with just extra-virgin olive oil, others with a lemon juice vinaigrette, still others are left plain. The salad makes a lovely first course when you're serving grilled lamb, or a nice light lunch, accompanied by crusty bread. The variation pictured at left (for nontraditionalists) includes lettuce.

SERVES 4 TO 6

2 tablespoons freshly squeezed lemon juice

Salt

Freshly ground black pepper

1 clove garlic, crushed

7 tablespoons extra-virgin olive oil

1 small green bell pepper, cored and sliced into thin rings

1 medium red onion, thinly sliced

2 cups ripe cherry tomatoes, halved

2 tablespoons capers, drained

1 cup Kalamata olives (about 30 medium)

1 medium seedless cucumber, peeled, cut into 1/2-inch cubes

1 cup diced feta cheese

1/4 cup chopped oregano

1/4 cup chopped parsley

4 scallions, light green and white parts only, cut on diagonal into 1/2-inch pieces

Combine the lemon juice, a generous pinch of salt, and several turns of the pepper mill in a small mixing bowl and stir to dissolve the salt. Add the garlic and olive oil and stir to combine; set aside for 30 minutes.

In a large salad bowl, combine all of the remaining ingredients and toss to combine. Remove and discard the garlic from the dressing, whisk to emulsify, and pour over the salad. Toss very gently just to coat, then transfer the salad to a large, deep platter; serve immediately.

napa cabbage and corn coleslaw
with honey-sage dressing

FULL OF COLOR, TEXTURE, and flavor, this appealing—and low-calorie—salad comes from chef Sue Chapman of The Lodge at Skylonda, a beautiful spa retreat sheltered under soaring redwood trees in the hills north of San Francisco. The dressing becomes even more aromatic if you add a few fresh lavender blossoms along with the sage.

SERVES 6

For the Dressing

2 tablespoons sage

1 tablespoon fresh lavender blossoms (optional)

2 cups nonfat plain yogurt

½ cup rice wine vinegar

4 tablespoons honey

4 tablespoons freshly squeezed lemon juice

1 teaspoon salt

½ teaspoon white pepper

For the Salad

2 ears fresh corn, husks removed

1 head napa cabbage, very thinly sliced

6 scallions, white and pale green parts only, chopped

1 large carrot, julienned

Make the dressing: In a small pot of boiling water, blanch the sage for 1 minute, drain, then slice into fine julienne. Combine all the ingredients in a blender, or the bowl of a small food processor, blend or process until smooth and emulsified, adjust the seasoning, then set aside.

Make the salad: Bring a large saucepan of water to a boil over high heat. Add the corn, and cook for 1 minute. Remove and immediately plunge into a cold water bath to stop the cooking. Drain and pat ears dry, then cut the corn kernels from the cob. Combine all the ingredients in a salad bowl. Briefly blend the dressing again to emulsify, then pour over the salad and toss to combine; serve immediately.

sliced cucumbers in
tarragon cream sauce

THIS LIGHT AND VERY SIMPLE VEGETABLE APPETIZER comes from French artist Aude Kamlet, who prepares it for summer lunches at her home in the bucolic Loire Valley countryside of Touraine with tarragon and cucumbers from her garden.

SERVES 6

3 tablespoons freshly squeezed lemon juice

Salt

Freshly ground black pepper

$\frac{3}{4}$ cup crème fraîche or sour cream

3 tablespoons chopped tarragon

2 long seedless cucumbers, thinly sliced into rounds

In a small bowl, combine the lemon juice and a generous pinch of salt and pepper, and stir to dissolve the salt. Add the crème fraîche and stir to blend. Stir in 2 tablespoons of the tarragon and set aside for 15 minutes to allow the flavors to develop. Arrange the cucumbers in concentric circles on a platter, spoon the tarragon cream over them, sprinkle on the remaining tarragon to garnish, and serve. (You can also combine the cucumbers and the tarragon cream in a salad bowl, toss gently to combine, and serve on individual plates, each sprinkled with a bit of chopped tarragon.)

dark opal basil oil
and variations

THERE ARE A VARIETY OF METHODS used to create an herb-infused olive oil. In one, you briefly heat the oil and the herbs together; in another, you blanch the herbs in boiling water, drain and dry them, puree them with the oil, and eventually strain the oil. Finally, there's the easiest and gentlest method, my preference, in which you simply combine the oil with the herbs, and whatever other flavorings you want to use, in a jar, seal it, and store it away in a cool, dark place for about 2 weeks. The herbs infuse the oil with no outside help at all, creating a lovely oil permeated with the essence of fresh herb. The recipe below is for an oil made with dark opal basil, which yields an aromatic, amethyst-hued oil, excellent on salads, drizzled over focaccia or sliced tomatoes, in marinades, or tossed with pasta. You can also make it with common sweet basil, as in the photograph on the right. Other variations follow.

MAKES 2 ¼ CUPS

1 cup dark opal basil, leaves and small stems
1 clove garlic, crushed
2 cups extra-virgin olive oil

Put the basil, garlic, and oil in a clean glass pint jar (an old mayonnaise jar works well). Cover the top of the jar with plastic wrap, seal tightly with the lid, and set aside in a cool, dark place, rocking the bottle back and forth from time to time, for 2 weeks. Strain, discarding the solids, then pour the oil into small, clean glass bottles. Seal the bottle with a cork or other nonmetallic cap. Store in the refrigerator, and use within 2 months.

VARIATIONS

Instead of the basil and garlic, combine the oil with 4 sprigs thyme, 3 sprigs rosemary, 1 bay leaf, and 6 peppercorns. This is a delicious oil in which to sauté chicken or veal.

Instead of the basil, combine the oil with the crushed garlic clove, 1 cup dill, 1 bay leaf, and 6 peppercorns. Use this, combined with a splash of lemon juice and some salt and pepper, to drizzle on grilled fish.

dilled mayonnaise

THIS IS A VERSATILE, EASY-TO-MAKE SAUCE infused with the aniselike flavor of fresh dill and brightened with a splash of lime. Use it as an accompaniment to cold poached salmon or steamed shrimp; as a sauce served with cold green beans or sliced cucumbers; or as a dressing for a potato salad, tossed with tiny boiled new potatoes after they cool. If you are adept at making your own mayonnaise, by all means make it for this recipe. Otherwise, a commercial brand such as Hellmann's works well.

MAKES ABOUT 1 1/2 CUPS

1 cup mayonnaise
1 rounded teaspoon Dijon mustard
2 teaspoons freshly squeezed lime juice
1 teaspoon minced onion
1/2 cup finely chopped dill
Salt
Freshly ground black pepper

In a mixing bowl, combine the mayonnaise, mustard, lime juice, onion, dill, a pinch of salt, and several turns of the pepper mill, then whisk briskly until all ingredients are incorporated and the sauce is smooth. Cover with plastic wrap and refrigerate at least 2 hours, or even overnight, before serving.

tarragon vinegar
and variations

ALL KINDS OF HERB COMBINATIONS can flavor vinegar beautifully, but one of the most traditional, aromatic, and best-flavored vinegars is the simple, noble tarragon vinegar. The recipe below calls for white wine vinegar, but you can also use basic white vinegar or rice wine vinegar. Using this method, you can make other flavored vinegars by substituting dill, chives, or basil for the tarragon. When using more assertive herbs, such as rosemary, thyme, or oregano, you should substitute red wine vinegar for the white wine vinegar.

MAKES 2 ¼ CUPS

1 cup tarragon, leaves and slim stems, lightly crushed in your hands
1 clove garlic, halved
2 cups white wine vinegar
Sprigs of tarragon (optional)

Put the tarragon and garlic in a clean glass pint jar (an old mayonnaise jar works well). Pour the vinegar into the jar, making sure that the tarragon is completely covered. Cover the top of the jar with plastic wrap, seal tightly with the lid, and set aside in a cool, dark place to infuse for about 2 weeks. Strain, discarding the solids, then pour the vinegar into small, clean glass bottles. Insert a fresh sprig of tarragon, making sure the vinegar covers the sprig. Seal the bottle with a cork or other nonmetallic cap, and store in a cool spot, away from sunlight.

VARIATIONS

To make a raspberry-thyme vinegar (very nice for gift-giving), replace the tarragon and garlic with ½ cup raspberries and 6 sprigs thyme. After 2 weeks, when rebottling, strain, then add 3 small sprigs thyme and 6 raspberries to each bottle before sealing.

To make a vinegar Provençal, replace the tarragon with 6 sprigs rosemary, 6 sprigs thyme, 1 bay leaf, and use 2 lightly crushed garlic cloves. Replace the white wine vinegar with red wine vinegar. This vinegar is delicious as part of a vinaigrette for a cold beef or lamb salad. You can also use it in a marinade for lamb, pork, or beef.

five-herb green rice salad

THIS IS ONE OF MY FAVORITE SALADS. I make it often in the summer, for picnics or barbecues, because it seems to complement almost everything I serve it with. The leafy herbs work in harmony with the onions and the flavorful green olives, the ensemble brightened by a generous portion of tangy lemon vinaigrette. The salad is delicious the day you make it (but let it chill in the refrigerator at for least two hours to let the flavors meld), as well as two or even three days later. Serve it in a clear glass salad bowl to maximize its allure.

SERVES 8 TO 10

3 cups long-grain rice

5 cups chicken stock

Salt

1/3 cup freshly squeezed lemon juice

3 tablespoons Dijon mustard

1 cup extra-virgin olive oil

1 cup Picholine olives, or other small green olives, pitted and halved

1 small red onion, diced

2 cups chopped curly parsley

1/2 cup chopped mint

1/2 cup chopped basil

1 tablespoon chopped marjoram

1 tablespoon finely julienned sage

Freshly ground black pepper

In a large saucepan, combine the rice, stock, and a pinch of salt, and bring to a boil over medium-high heat. Cover, lower the heat to low, and cook until all the liquid is absorbed, about 17 minutes. Remove from the heat, stir to fluff up the rice, cover again, and set aside to cool.

Meanwhile, in a small bowl, combine the lemon juice and 1/2 teaspoon salt and whisk to dissolve the salt. Add the mustard, whisk to blend, then add the olive oil and whisk to emulsify. Set aside.

In a large mixing bowl, combine the cooled rice, olives, onion, and all the herbs, and toss gently to combine. Whisk the vinaigrette to emulsify, then pour over the salad and toss gently to evenly coat the rice with dressing. Season with salt and several turns of the pepper mill to taste, cover with plastic wrap, and refrigerate for at least 2 hours. Just before serving, toss again to mix in the dressing, then transfer to a glass salad bowl; serve.

breads
and savory
tarts

broccoli rabe and potato torte
with thyme, oregano, and chives

IN THIS LUSCIOUS, SAVORY TORTE—similar to a pie, with flaky top and bottom crusts—French chef Denis Jaricot, of the sun-washed CuisinArt Resort in Anguilla, combines broccoli rabe, potatoes, and Parmigiano-Reggiano cheese with a trio of just-plucked herbs from the resort's unique hydroponic garden.

SERVES 6 TO 8

For the Crust
3 cups cake flour
1 teaspoon salt
2 large eggs
5 tablespoons unsalted butter,
   at room temperature

For the Filling
1 bunch broccoli rabe, leaves only
4 tablespoons extra-virgin olive oil
1 white onion, diced

3 large baking potatoes, peeled and cut
   into $1/4$-inch rounds
$1/4$ bunch thyme, leaves only
$1/4$ bunch oregano, leaves only
1 bunch chives
$1/2$ cup heavy cream
1 egg
$3/4$ cup freshly grated Parmigiano-Reggiano cheese
Salt
Freshly ground black pepper

Make the crust: Sift the flour and salt into a mixing bowl. Lightly beat the eggs in a small bowl and stir them into the flour mixture with a fork. Cut in the butter, and stir until the dough is crumbly and just holds together in a ball. Turn the dough out onto a lightly floured work surface and knead several times. Separate the dough into 2 equal balls and set aside.

Make the filling: Blanch the broccoli rabe in boiling water for 3 minutes; drain. In a large sauté pan heat half of the oil, add the onion, and sauté over medium heat for 2 minutes; add the potatoes and cook for 5 minutes; stir in the broccoli rabe and the herbs. Pour in the cream and bring to a boil, then remove from heat.

In a small bowl, lightly beat the egg. Transfer the potato mixture to a large bowl, and stir in the egg and the cheese. Add salt and pepper to taste.

Preheat the oven to 375° F. Roll the pastry dough into two rectangles (or circles, if you want to make the torte in a 10-inch round pie pan), about $1/8$ inch thick. Lightly oil a 12-inch baking dish and place one pastry sheet in the bottom and up the sides. Spread the potato mixture evenly in the pastry shell, place the second sheet over, and crimp the edges to seal. Trim off the excess dough. Prick the top of the torte several times with a fork, and drizzle the top with the remaining oil.

Bake for 45 minutes to 1 hour, until the crust is browned and begins to separate from the edge of the dish. Serve hot or at room temperature.

pissaladière

provençal onion and anchovy tart

THE PISSALADIÈRE, A TART THAT COMBINES caramelized onions, anchovies, herbs, and black olives on a breadlike dough, is a traditional baked treat from the southern part of Provence, particularly around the Mediterranean city of Nice. Although natives of Nice abhor comparisons of their pissaladière with pizza, which it visually resembles, you could successfully make a version of this tart with pizza dough.

SERVES 10 AS AN HORS D'OEUVRE; 6 AS AN APPETIZER

For the Crust
1½ teaspoons active dry yeast
1 cup flour
1 teaspoon salt
1 tablespoon olive oil

For the Topping
3 tablespoons olive oil, plus a little for garnish
6 medium onions, very thinly sliced

1 clove garlic, finely chopped
1 teaspoon thyme leaves
1 bay leaf
¼ teaspoon salt
¼ teaspoon freshly ground black pepper
About 20 small black Niçoise olives, pitted
¼ cup parsley leaves
6 anchovy fillets in oil, drained

Make the crust: In a medium mixing bowl, combine the yeast and ⅓ cup lukewarm water, stir, then set aside in a warm place for 5 to 10 minutes. Add the flour, salt, and oil, and mix to combine thoroughly. Turn out onto a floured work surface and knead for about 10 minutes, until the dough is soft, smooth, and elastic. Transfer the dough to a greased bowl, cover loosely with a damp towel or plastic wrap, and set aside to rise at room temperature for at least 1 hour.

Make the topping: In a large skillet, heat the 3 tablespoons of the oil over medium heat. Add the onions, garlic, thyme, bay leaf, salt, and pepper, and stir to combine. Lower the heat to low, and cook, stirring frequently, until the onions are soft, translucent, and slightly golden, about 45 minutes. Remove and discard

the bay leaf, and set the pan aside to cool.

Punch down the dough, then, on a floured work surface, working with a floured rolling pin, roll out the dough to a 12-inch circle about ¼ inch thick. Transfer the dough to a lightly greased baking sheet. Spread the onion mixture over the dough, leaving a ½-inch border. Scatter on the black olives, then set aside to rest for 15 minutes.

Preheat the oven to 375° F. Bake the tart in the center of the oven for 15 minutes. Scatter on the parsley leaves, and arrange the anchovy fillets in a spoke pattern on the surface of the tart. Bake for another 15 minutes or so, until the edges of the tart are nicely browned. Remove from the oven, drizzle a little bit of oil over the tart, cut into wedges, and serve immediately.

cheddar-dill scones

I LOVE ALL KINDS OF SCONES, both savory and sweet, and I serve them often—at brunch or tea with golden raisins or currants, berries or apricot bits; at buffet lunches or dinners with herbs and perhaps cheese. The fruit scones I make round, but savory ones like these I cut into small wedges before baking, and serve them in a rustic basket lined with a pretty napkin.

MAKES ABOUT 12 SCONES

3 cups flour

2 tablespoons sugar

3 teaspoons salt

1 tablespoon plus 1 teaspoon baking powder

$\frac{1}{3}$ cup coarsely chopped dill

$1\frac{1}{3}$ cups finely shredded sharp cheddar cheese

$1\frac{2}{3}$ cups heavy cream

Preheat the oven to 425° F. Sift the flour, sugar, salt, and baking powder into a large mixing bowl. Whisk together to combine. Add the dill and 1 cup of the cheese, and whisk to combine. Add the cream, and, using a wooden spoon, stir until the dough comes together but is still lumpy.

Knead the dough gently, pressing it against the side of the bowl about 10 times. Transfer the dough to a floured work surface and pat it into a slightly domed 10-inch disk. Cut into 12 to 16 narrow wedges and transfer to an ungreased baking sheet, about 1 inch apart. Sprinkle the tops with the remaining cheese and bake for 12 to 15 minutes, until lightly browned on top. Transfer to a wire rack. Serve warm or at room temperature.

easy rosemary focaccia

FOCACCIA IS A CLASSIC SAVORY ITALIAN BREAD, flat and yeasty and generously dosed with olive oil. Traditionally it requires several hours preparation time—proofing, kneading, rising, punching down, rising, again and again. This recipe is a simplified version of the bread, more elaborate than pizza bread, less involved than classic focaccia. The dough is scented with rosemary. In addition to garnishing with rosemary and salt, you can also top this with little bacon bits— 2 ounces slab bacon, finely chopped, then lightly browned—sprinkled on just before baking, along with the rosemary and salt.

SERVES 6 TO 8

One $\frac{1}{4}$-ounce package (1 scant tablespoon)
  active dry yeast
$3\frac{3}{4}$ cups flour
$\frac{1}{2}$ cup olive oil
1 tablespoon fine sea salt

1 teaspoon sugar
1 tablespoon minced rosemary
1 tablespoon coarsely chopped rosemary
1 teaspoon coarse sea salt

Combine the yeast and $1\frac{1}{3}$ cups warm water in a small bowl and stir to dissolve. Set aside for 5 minutes. Combine the flour, 2 tablespoons of the oil, the finely ground salt, sugar, and minced rosemary in a large bowl. Add the yeast mixture and stir with a wooden spoon to blend. Knead for 10 minutes by hand, or knead in the bowl of an electric mixer equipped with a dough hook until smooth and elastic. Brush the inside of a large clean bowl with oil, transfer the dough to the bowl, and press it against the bottom and sides of the bowl to coat thoroughly with oil. Cover with plastic wrap, so that the wrap covers the surface of the dough, and set aside to rise until it doubles in volume, about $1\frac{1}{2}$ hours.

Punch down the dough. On a floured work surface, press it into a rough rectangle, 9 by 12 inches. With a rolling pin, roll out the dough to a 10- by 14-inch rectangle. Line a 10- by 14-inch baking pan with kitchen parchment. Brush the parchment and the sides of the pan with oil. Gently transfer the dough to the pan, and stretch it out to the edges of the pan. Brush the top of the dough with oil, cover with plastic wrap, and set aside to rise for $1\frac{1}{2}$ hours.

Preheat the oven to 400° F. Five minutes before baking, press "dimples" in the dough with your fingertips, about $\frac{3}{4}$ inch deep, 2 inches apart. Drizzle the remaining oil (about $\frac{1}{3}$ cup) over the dough, then sprinkle with chopped rosemary and coarse salt. Bake on the center rack of the oven for 20 minutes, then lower the heat to 350° F and bake for another 25 minutes, or until the top is crisp and golden brown. Cool in the pan for 10 to 15 minutes, then transfer to a wire rack.

Serve warm or at room temperature. Cut into squares.

fromage blanc and potato tart
with thyme and caramelized onions

THIS RICH, DELICIOUS, AND UNUSUAL TART, layering caramelized onions, fromage blanc, and thinly sliced potatoes, was created by Max London, a chef and talented young baker from a family of talented bakers. Max is the son of Mark and Wendy London, founders of the notable Mrs. London's Bakery in Saratoga Springs, New York, a wonderful country bakery with a national reputation for excellence. *Food and Wine* magazine hailed it recently as "the country's most fabulous bakeshop." In Max's tart, the distinctive flavor of thyme, mixed with the fromage blanc, permeates the tart. Fromage blanc is a creamy, tangy, French-style cheese product resembling sour cream in appearance, but with little or no fat content (mail-order sources are listed in the back of this book). If you cannot obtain fromage blanc, substitute a 50/50 combination of ricotta and whipped cream cheese. The texture of the tart with ricotta and whipped cream will be a little less creamy and more dense than Max's original (and the fat content significantly higher), but it is good in its own right. You will need a 10 ½-inch, removable-bottom tart pan.

SERVES 6 TO 8

For the Pastry Shell

1 scant cup all-purpose flour

4 tablespoons potato starch

5 tablespoons unsalted butter

¼ teaspoon sea salt

2 large egg yolks

For the Filling

4 tablespoons unsalted butter

4 large onions, halved and very thinly sliced

2 cups fromage blanc (10% or more fat content
   is preferable to nonfat in this recipe);
   or 1 cup whole milk ricotta blended with
   1 cup whipped cream cheese

2 egg yolks

2½ tablespoons cake flour

1 cup heavy cream

¼ cup coarsely chopped fresh thyme

2 large egg whites

1½ large (or 2 medium) baking potatoes,
   peeled and very thinly sliced

Sea salt

Freshly ground black pepper

Make the pastry shell: In the bowl of a food processor, combine the all-purpose flour, potato starch, butter, and salt, and pulse until the mixture resembles coarse sand. Add the egg yolks and 3 tablespoons cold water and process just until the mixture starts to come together in a ball. The mixture should be satiny and slightly elastic to the touch; if the mixture seems too stiff, add another tablespoon or so of water and pulse to incorporate. Remove the dough from the bowl, and knead it in your hands for about 3 minutes; it should be smooth and malleable, and not at all sticky; if it is a little sticky, flour your hands and continue to knead until the stickiness disappears. Press the dough into a flat disk, wrap in plastic wrap, and refrigerate for about 30 minutes.

On a floured work surface, using a floured rolling pin, roll out the dough to a 13-inch circle. Carefully lifting the dough by draping it over the rolling pin, transfer it to a 10½-inch, removable-bottom tart pan. Press the dough into the bottom and sides of the pan, and trim the dough, leaving about ½ inch overhanging. Fold this overhang onto the dough at the top of the rim, and crimp the border. Pierce the dough in several places on the bottom and sides with the tines of a fork, cover lightly with plastic wrap, and refrigerate until ready to use.

Make the filling: In a large skillet over medium heat, melt 2 tablespoons of the butter. Add the onions and cook, stirring frequently, until soft and caramelized, about 20 minutes. Remove the skillet from the heat and set aside.

Meanwhile, preheat the oven to 400° F. In the bowl of an electric mixer, or a mixing bowl, combine the fromage blanc, egg yolks, cake flour, cream, and thyme. Season the mixture liberally with salt (I use about 2 teaspoons) and pepper (about ½ teaspoon). Mix until smooth and thoroughly blended. In another bowl, beat the egg whites until they hold soft peaks, then fold them into the fromage blanc mixture.

Spread the onions over the base of the tart shell, and press lightly. Pour the fromage blanc mixture over the onions and smooth the top. Bake until the mixture just begins to get firm, about 12 minutes. Meanwhile, in a small skillet or in a microwave oven, melt the remaining 2 tablespoons butter, pour over the sliced potatoes, and toss to coat the slices. After the tart has baked for about 12 minutes, remove it from the oven and layer the buttered potato slices over the top in a pattern of concentric circles, working from the outside in. Drizzle any remaining melted butter from the potatoes over the top, and season with salt and pepper. Return to the oven and bake until the top is light golden brown and the filling is set, about 45 minutes. Transfer to a wire rack to cool slightly. Serve warm.

provençal tomato tartlets

THE MAS DE CORNUD IS A HANDSOME STONE COUNTRY INN surrounded by vegetable gardens, vineyards, and fields of lavender in the sun-bathed Provençal countryside near Saint-Rémy-de-Provence. The large farmhouse, built in the 1700s, was converted into an inn and cooking school in the mid-1980s by David Carpita, a former investment banker, and his wife, Nito, a chef and cooking school instructor. At the Mas de Cornud students enjoy a memorable, weeklong introduction to Provençal cuisine and lifestyle. Menus and recipes change from week to week, but courses include such dishes as this easy-to-assemble tomato tartlet redolent with rosemary, sage, basil, and garlic. I like to serve these on small, rustic wooden cutting boards garnished with sprigs of fresh herbs. As a variation, you can substitute small red and yellow tomatoes for the plum tomatoes.

SERVES 6

2 sheets frozen puff pastry (one 17-ounce package)
$\frac{1}{2}$ cup olive oil
1 medium onion, diced
4 cloves garlic, minced
2 pounds plum tomatoes, peeled, seeded, and chopped
3 sage leaves, sliced into fine julienne
1 sprig rosemary, broken in two
6 to 8 plum tomatoes, thinly sliced crosswise
Salt
Freshly ground black pepper
2 tablespoons minced basil
6 sprigs basil (optional)

Remove the puff pastry from the freezer, unwrap, and allow it to come to room temperature; set aside. In a medium skillet, heat 3 tablespoons of the oil over medium heat. Add the onion and half the garlic, lower the heat to medium-low, and cook until the onion is translucent, about 4 minutes. Do not let the onion or garlic brown. Add the chopped tomatoes, sage, and rosemary and stir to combine. Simmer for about 30 minutes, until the mixture is reduced by almost half. Remove from the heat and set aside.

Preheat the oven to 375° F. On a well-floured work surface, using a floured rolling pin, roll out the sheets of puff pastry to a thickness of $\frac{1}{16}$ inch; their surface area should increase by almost half. Using a 7-inch bowl or plate as a guide, cut out 3 rounds from each pastry sheet. Transfer the rounds to two ungreased baking sheets, three on each. (If you only have one baking sheet, or a small oven, bake the tartlets in two batches.)

Spread 2 tablespoons of the tomato mixture over each pastry round, leaving a $\frac{1}{2}$-inch border on the outside edge. Arrange the tomato slices on the top of each tartlet, one small slice in the center and an overlapping circle of tomatoes around it. Season each tartlet with a pinch of salt and several turns of the pepper mill. Bake in the center of the oven for about 15 minutes, until the crusts are golden brown. Remove and transfer to a wire rack to cool slightly.

In a small bowl, combine the minced basil and the remaining garlic. Gradually whisk in the remaining olive oil. Transfer the tartlets to individual plates, drizzle each tartlet with 1 tablespoon of the basil-oil mixture, garnish with sprigs of basil if you wish, and serve immediately.

goat cheese and herb frittata

THIS COLORFUL FLAT OMELET, studded with a mélange of fresh herbs and tangy with the wonderful flavor of creamy, young goat cheese, can be eaten hot at brunch or a light lunch, or cold at a picnic. It cooks partially on the stove top, and finishes in the oven.

SERVES 4 TO 6

1 pound asparagus, stalks trimmed 3 inches from tip,
then each 3-inch piece halved; discard bottoms

8 eggs

$\frac{1}{4}$ teaspoon salt

Freshly ground black pepper

3 tablespoons chopped basil

2 tablespoons chopped scallions or chives

2 tablespoons chopped parsley

2 tablespoons chopped tarragon

$\frac{1}{3}$ cup chèvre goat cheese

3 tablespoons unsalted butter

Preheat the oven to 375° F. Bring a medium pot of water to boil over high heat. Add the asparagus, lower the heat to medium, and cook for about 2 minutes, until the asparagus pieces are crisp-tender. Drain, then plunge into a bowl of cold water. Drain again, and set aside.

In a large mixing bowl, combine the eggs, salt, and 8 to 10 generous turns of the pepper mill, and beat for about 10 seconds. Add the basil, scallions, parsley, and tarragon, and beat to combine. Spoon in the chèvre in small bits, then beat to slightly combine. Little bits of cheese will be distributed throughout the egg mixture but should not be blended in. Stir in the asparagus.

In a large oven-proof skillet, melt the butter over medium-high heat. Pour in the egg mixture, using a spatula to spread the asparagus and cheese bits evenly over the surface. Reduce heat to medium and cook for about 3 minutes, until the edges of the frittata just begin to firm and bubble. Transfer the pan to the oven, and cook about 4 minutes, just until the top of the frittata is firm and puffy. Do not overcook. Remove from the oven, loosen the bottom of the omelet with a spatula, then slide the omelet onto a large, warmed platter and serve immediately, cut into wedges. If serving cold, slide the omelet onto an unwarmed platter, let cool, then cover with plastic wrap and refrigerate until ready to serve.

roquefort- and herb-stuffed eggs

DEVILED EGGS AND OTHER VERSIONS OF STUFFED EGGS have been out of culinary fashion for a couple of decades, but whenever I serve them, at a brunch, on a buffet table, or as hors d'oeuvres, they are always among the first things to disappear. Make them about 2 hours ahead, then refrigerate; remove them from the refrigerator about 20 minutes before serving. For a more festive presentation, garnish the platter with sprigs of herbs and thin slices of lemon.

SERVES 8

8 eggs

4 tablespoons Roquefort or Danish blue cheese, crumbled

$1/4$ cup mayonnaise

1 tablespoon Dijon mustard

1 teaspoon minced shallots

2 tablespoons chopped, plus 1 tablespoon very finely minced scallions or chives

1 teaspoon thyme, crushed

$1/2$ teaspoon Worcestershire sauce

Freshly ground black pepper

Salt

Paprika (optional)

Bring a large saucepan of water to a boil over high heat. Using a slotted spoon, or a tablespoon, lower the eggs into the water. When the water just comes to a boil again, lower the heat to medium, and simmer for 15 minutes. Drain the eggs, then, while they are still in the saucepan, run them under cold water for 1 minute to stop the cooking, then let them sit in the cold water until cool.

Peel the shells off, then slice the eggs in half lengthwise. Scoop out the yolks and put them in a small mixing bowl, and arrange the whites on a platter. Using the tines of a fork, mash the yolks until they have the consistency of coarse sand. Then add the cheese, mayonnaise, mustard, shallot, 2 tablespoons chopped scallions, thyme, Worcestershire sauce, and several generous turns of the pepper mill. Using a fork or a small wire whisk, mix and mash the ingredients until smoothly incorporated. Taste, then add salt if needed; both the Roquefort cheese and the Worcestershire sauce are salty, so typically little salt is needed.

Using a teaspoon, spoon the yolk mixture onto the centers of the whites, and gently mound, then garnish the tops of the eggs with the minced scallion. Sprinkle with a dusting of paprika, if you wish, then cover lightly with plastic wrap and refrigerate until ready to serve. Remove from the refrigerator about 20 minutes before serving.

omelet with *fines herbes*

EGGS ARE ONE OF THE KITCHEN'S MOST ADAPTABLE mediums, lending themselves to an infinite number of ingredient combinations and preparation techniques. They can be flat or fluffy, dense or cloudlike, intensely flavored in an appetizer, sweet and ethereal in a dessert. Here, with three delicate, aromatic green herbs and a bit of butter and salt, they compose a classic French omelet, one of the very best things you can do with eggs—and with herbs.

SERVES 2

2 tablespoons finely chopped chives
1 tablespoon finely chopped tarragon
1 tablespoon finely chopped parsley
4 tablespoons unsalted butter
5 eggs
Sea salt
Freshly ground black pepper

Combine the chives, tarragon, and parsley in a small bowl. In an 8- to 10-inch omelet pan, melt 1 tablespoon of the butter over medium-high heat. When it stops bubbling, add the herbs and stir into the butter. Cook for 30 seconds, stirring constantly, then remove from the heat and set aside.

In a medium-sized bowl, combine the eggs, a generous pinch of salt, and four or five turns of the pepper mill. Beat just until the eggs are uniformly combined. Add the herb mixture from the pan, and beat just three or four strokes, until combined. Melt the remaining butter in the omelet pan over medium-high heat. When the butter stops bubbling, pour in the egg mixture. Let it cook without disturbing it for at least 30 seconds. When the edges appear firm and dry, gently lift the edge of the omelet away from the side of the pan and tilt the pan slightly so uncooked portions from the center of the omelet flow underneath. Continue lifting the edges at different places on the omelet until the top is just set and still creamy. Using a spatula, gently lift half of the omelet and fold it over the other half. Gently slide the omelet out of the pan onto a warmed plate and serve immediately.

VARIATION: You can use this same recipe to make a sorrel omelet, a tasty variation with a pleasingly sour tang. Omit the herbs and cook $\frac{1}{4}$ pound sorrel in 3 tablespoons butter for about 8 minutes, until sorrel wilts. Then stir it into beaten eggs. Use 3 tablespoons butter to cook the omelet.

vegetables

cremini mushrooms
and herb sauté

IN THIS EASY-TO-PREPARE RECIPE, a perfect accompaniment for grilled steak or roast chicken, the rich, earthy flavor of the mushrooms is balanced by the clean, green flavor of the flat-leaf parsley.

SERVES 4

3 tablespoons olive oil

2 cloves garlic, finely chopped

1 pound cremini mushrooms, stems trimmed to $\frac{1}{2}$ inch from cap, cut into $\frac{1}{4}$-inch slices

$\frac{1}{3}$ cup firmly packed flat-leaf parsley, tops only, chopped

$\frac{3}{4}$ teaspoon coarse salt

Coarsely ground black pepper

In a large skillet, heat the olive oil over medium heat. Add the garlic and cook for 1 minute, stirring constantly to keep the garlic from browning. Add the mushrooms, stir to coat with oil, and cook, stirring frequently, until the mushrooms begin to give off their liquid, 5 to 7 minutes. Add the parsley and stir to combine, then add the salt and 6 or 7 turns of the pepper mill. Cook for 2 minutes longer, stirring frequently, then remove from the heat and serve immediately on warmed plates.

rosemary gnocchi

THESE DELICIOUS GNOCCHI ARE THE CREATION of chef Oliver Dudler of New York's Peninsula Hotel. He serves them in the autumn as an accompaniment to a succulent main course of pan-seared venison medallions and braised figs, but they are also ideal with any rich roast, such as roast beef or leg of lamb.

SERVES 4 TO 6

1 pound Idaho potatoes
Salt
$\frac{1}{2}$ cup flour
$\frac{1}{2}$ cup freshly grated Parmigiano cheese
$\frac{1}{2}$ cup rosemary, minced
1 large egg
$1\frac{1}{2}$ teaspoons salt
$\frac{1}{2}$ teaspoon freshly ground black pepper
1 tablespoon unsalted butter

Boil the potatoes, with the skin on, in salted water until soft. Drain and set aside until cool enough to handle. Peel the potatoes and, while still warm, mash until smooth. Add the flour, cheese, rosemary, egg, salt, and pepper, mixing until thoroughly blended and a soft dough forms.

Divide the dough into 8 equal portions. Roll each portion on a lightly floured surface into a rope about $\frac{1}{2}$ inch thick and 16 inches long. Cut the rope on a bias into $1\frac{1}{2}$-inch pieces, forming diamond-shaped gnocchi. Boil in a pot of salted boiling water until they float to the top. Remove, cool in an ice bath, drain, and place on a baking sheet lined with paper towels. Cover with plastic wrap and store in the refrigerator until ready to serve.

Place the butter in a large sauté pan or skillet over medium-high heat and cook until it is lightly browned. Add the gnocchi and cook until heated through and very lightly browned. Blot dry with a paper towel. Spoon onto warmed individual plates as a side dish, or transfer to a warmed serving bowl and serve at the table.

herbed linguine primavera

THE SCAGLIO FAMILY HAS HAD A FINE produce and meat market in the village of Katonah, New York, for almost thirty years. Run today by John Scaglio and his son, Michael, the market features, in addition to high-quality meats, vegetables, and fruit, flavorful prepared dishes created from old family recipes. One of them is this fresh and colorful linguine primavera enhanced by generous amounts of fresh parsley and basil.

SERVES 4 AS AN APPETIZER, 2 AS A MAIN COURSE

$^1\!/_2$ pound linguine

1 cup chicken stock

2 teaspoons cornstarch

2 tablespoons olive oil

2 cloves garlic, minced

$^1\!/_2$ pound fresh asparagus, ends trimmed,
   cut into 1-inch pieces

2 medium carrots, very thinly sliced on the bias

1 medium onion, chopped

6 ounces fresh peas in the pod

$^2\!/_3$ cup sliced almonds or chopped cashews
   (optional)

$^1\!/_3$ cup chopped parsley leaves

3 tablespoons julienned basil

1 teaspoon finely julienned sage

Freshly ground black pepper

$^1\!/_2$ cup freshly grated Parmigiano-Reggiano cheese

Cook the linguine according to the directions on the package, then drain.

Meanwhile, prepare the sauce: In a small bowl, combine the stock and the cornstarch and stir to dissolve the cornstarch; set aside. Heat the oil in a large skillet over medium-high heat, add the garlic, and cook, stirring constantly so that it doesn't burn, for about 15 seconds. Add the asparagus, carrots, and onion, and cook, stirring constantly, for about 2 minutes. Add the pea pods, almonds, parsley, basil, sage, and pepper to taste. Cook for about 1 minute longer, until the vegetables are crisp-tender. Transfer the vegetables to a warmed bowl and set aside.

Stir the stock mixture to make sure the cornstarch is thoroughly blended, then pour into the skillet. Bring to a boil over medium-high heat, stirring constantly. When the mixture has thickened, after 1 to 2 minutes, return the vegetable mixture to the skillet and stir to coat with the sauce. Season to taste with salt and pepper. Lower the heat to medium and cook just until vegetables are heated through, 1 to 2 minutes. Place the hot linguine in a large warmed serving bowl or platter. Spoon the vegetable mixture over the linguini, sprinkle with the cheese, and serve immediately.

bouquet of autumn root vegetables
with green herb sauce

ONE OF THE MANY PLEASURES OF A VISIT to the beautiful Hotel Meurice on the rue de Rivoli in Paris, is dining in the opulent, eighteenth-century-style dining room of Le Meurice restaurant, facing the Tuileries Gardens. Here chef Marc Marchand creates inventive and visually striking cuisine that changes with the seasons. His bouquet of autumn root vegetables is a lovely, light side dish that features carrots, salsify, chervil root, Jerusalem artichoke, celery root, beets, and turnips. The vegetables are all whittled into little cork shapes and arranged separately on a plate, almost like an artist's palette, surrounding a deep green pool of intensely flavored herb sauce. This recipe is an adaptation of Marchand's dish, using four root vegetables, but you could certainly add more if you wish. If chervil is unavailable, substitute ¾ cup of chopped chives and add an additional ¼ cup parsley.

SERVES 6

For the Vegetables

1 pound carrots, peeled and sliced into
 ¾-inch rounds
1 pound celery root, peeled and cut into
 1½-inch cubes
1 pound beets, leaves trimmed off, scrubbed
1 pound turnips, peeled and cut into
 ¾-inch rounds
2 cups, or more, chicken stock
Salt
4 tablespoons unsalted butter

For the Herb Sauce

2 cups firmly packed watercress,
 leaves and top half of stems only

1 cup firmly packed chervil, leaves and
 small stems only
½ cup firmly packed Italian parsley, leaves
 and small stems only
½ cup firmly packed tarragon, leaves
 and small stems only
5 leaves lemon balm (optional)
½ cup reserved chicken stock
 from vegetables, warmed
½ cup extra-virgin olive oil
2 teaspoons freshly squeezed lemon juice
½ teaspoon salt
Freshly ground black pepper

6 small herb bouquets, tied with parsley stems,
 for garnish

Cook each of the vegetables separately using the following method: Put the vegetables in a small skillet with enough stock to cover the vegetables halfway, and add a pinch of salt. Bring to a boil over high heat, add 1 tablespoon butter, lower the heat to medium, cover, and cook until the vegetables are just tender when pierced with the tip of a knife. Approximate cooking times for each vegetable are: carrots, 5 minutes; celery root, 8 minutes; beets, 30 minutes; turnips, 8 minutes. Drain each vegetable, reserving the stock. When the beets are cooked, peel them and cut into large cubes. Transfer the vegetables, each in a separate mound, to a large platter, lightly cover with aluminum foil, and keep warm in the oven on its lowest setting.

Make the herb sauce: Bring a large saucepan of water to a boil over high heat. Add the watercress, chervil, parsley, tarragon, and lemon balm and boil just 1 minute. Remove from the heat, drain the herbs, and immediately plunge them into a large bowl of ice water. Transfer the herbs to a blender or small food processor, add the reserved stock and puree. Add the oil, lemon juice, salt, and 8 to 10 turns of the pepper mill, and puree until the mixture is smoothly blended. Taste and adjust the seasoning, if necessary, then transfer the mixture to a saucepan and warm over medium heat just before serving.

Divide the vegetables among 6 warmed serving plates, arranging each vegetable separately around the outside edge of the plates, creating 4 "quadrants" framing a space in the center. Spoon a generous amount of the herb sauce into the center of each plate, garnish with the herb bouquets, and serve immediately.

grilled corn
with lemon-chive butter

DELICIOUS WITH CORN GRILLED ON THE BARBECUE, the lemon-chive butter in this recipe is also excellent with steamed or boiled corn.

SERVES 6

2 tablespoons freshly squeezed lemon juice

$1/4$ teaspoon salt

$1/2$ cup unsalted butter, softened

1 teaspoon grated lemon zest

$1/4$ cup finely chopped chives

6 ears fresh corn, in the husks

In a small glass or ceramic bowl, combine the lemon juice and the salt and whisk to dissolve the salt. Add the butter, lemon zest, and chives, and beat together to cream the butter. Cover with plastic wrap and refrigerate until ready to use.

Draw back the husks of the corn, remove the silks, then smooth the husks back into place. Place the ears in a large pot, fill to cover with cold water, and soak for 30 minutes. Drain and pat dry. Prepare a charcoal fire; when the coals are ready—hot, red inside, with a soft covering of gray ash—place the ears, still in their husks, on the grill, about 5 inches from the coals. Grill for about 15 minutes, until the husks are charred and the corn kernels are tender. Remove the charred husks, spread each ear with lemon-chive butter, arrange on a platter, and serve immediately.

provençal braised summer vegetables

THE ROMANTIC AND BEAUTIFUL Hostellerie de l'Abbaye de la Celle, in the Provençal village of La Celle, near Brignoles, is a former convent gorgeously restored by world-renowned French chef Alain Ducasse and recently opened as a dreamlike French country inn. Here one of his top chefs, Benoît Witz, formerly of Le Louis XV in Monte Carlo, creates generous, refined country-style meals that take full advantage of the superb local produce. In this dish, which you could serve as a first course, or as an accompaniment to braised beef or roasted chicken, rabbit, or veal, the bright, fresh summer vegetables are given savory depth by the addition of the large herb bouquet, the chopped slab bacon, and the rich chicken stock.

SERVES 4

$1/2$ lemon

10 baby purple artichokes

1 medium head garlic

4 small zucchini, about 1 inch in diameter, skin sliced into strips about
$3/4$-inch wide and $1/4$-inch thick; discard interior

3 tablespoons olive oil

2 ounces slab bacon, coarsely chopped

8 young carrots, peeled, tops trimmed to 1 inch

4 white baby onions, peeled and trimmed

1 large sprig each of basil, parsley, chervil, and chives, tied with string into a bouquet

1 cup dry white wine

1 cup full-flavored chicken stock

6 zucchini blossoms (optional)

Salt

Freshly ground black pepper

Fill a medium bowl half full of cold water. Squeeze the lemon half over the water, then drop it into the water. Remove the tough outer leaves of the artichokes by snapping them off at the base, exposing the pale yellow interior leaves. Cut off the top third of the artichokes, trim the stems to 1 inch, then peel off the outer skin of the stems with a vegetable peeler. As soon as it's prepared, place each artichoke in the bowl of lemon-water.

Peel all but the last, thin, translucent layer of skin from the garlic and separate the cloves; set aside. With a paring knife, cut the zucchini skin into 1-inch "chips"; set aside.

In a large casserole, heat the oil over medium heat. Add the artichokes and the bacon and cook, stirring frequently, for 5 minutes. Add the carrots and the onions and cook for 3 minutes, stirring frequently, for 5 minutes. Add the garlic and herb bouquet and stir to combine. Add the wine and cook until the liquid is reduced by two-thirds. Add the stock, lower the heat to medium-low, and cook for about 15 minutes, until the artichokes and carrots are tender when pierced with the tip of a knife. Add the zucchini and cook for 2 minutes. Add the zucchini blossoms, if using, cook for 1 minute, then remove from the heat. Season to taste with salt and pepper, then divide the vegetables and sauce equally among 4 serving bowls. Serve immediately.

glazed carrots with mint

SWEET AND DELICATELY MINTY, this carrot dish is a nice accompaniment to a pot roast or sauerbraten.

SERVES 6

6 tablespoons unsalted butter
1 medium onion, diced
1$\frac{1}{2}$ pounds carrots, scraped and sliced into $\frac{1}{4}$-inch rounds
$\frac{1}{4}$ teaspoon salt
3 tablespoons light brown sugar
2 tablespoons chopped mint

In a medium skillet, melt 3 tablespoons of the butter over medium heat. Add the onion and cook, stirring occasionally, until the onion softens and begins to become translucent, about 4 minutes. Add the carrots, and stir to coat with butter. Add 1$\frac{1}{4}$ cups water and the salt, and stir to combine. When the liquid comes to a boil, cover the pan, lower the heat to medium-low, and cook, maintaining a gentle simmer, until the carrots are just tender, 20 to 30 minutes.

Uncover, add the remaining 3 tablespoons butter, and stir to melt and combine. Add the brown sugar and the mint and stir to combine. Cook, stirring frequently, until the carrots are nicely glazed with the sauce, 3 to 4 minutes. Adjust the seasoning, then transfer to a warmed serving dish and serve immediately.

steamed new potatoes
with fresh herbs

THIS IS A VERY SIMPLE AND ATTRACTIVE WAY to prepare a side dish of steamed new potatoes. The recipe comes from John and Michael Scaglio, owners of Scaglio's Marketplace in the charming village of Katonah, New York, who always have fine suggestions for preparing their excellent produce and meats.

SERVES 4 TO 6

1$\frac{1}{2}$ pounds new red potatoes, scrubbed but not peeled

4 tablespoons unsalted butter, softened

2 teaspoons chopped chervil

2 teaspoons chopped chives

2 teaspoons chopped parsley

2 teaspoons chopped tarragon

Coarse salt

Coarsely ground black pepper

Place the potatoes in the top of a double boiler set over 1 to 2 inches of boiling water, or in a stainless steel basket set over a large saucepan of boiling water. Cover and steam until the potatoes are tender and can be easily pierced with the tip of a paring knife, 15 to 20 minutes. Transfer to a colander and let drain and dry for about 5 minutes. Place the butter in a shallow bowl, and the herbs in another bowl. Using a tablespoon, or your fingers if the potatoes are not too hot, roll each potato in the butter to coat, then roll in the herbs to coat, and place in a warmed serving bowl. Sprinkle them with a bit of salt and pepper, and any herbs remaining in the bowl, and serve immediately.

chive-chervil mashed potatoes

CHIVE AND CHERVIL ARE TWO DELICATE *fines herbes* that work beautifully in tandem. In this recipe they are warmed in melted butter, then stirred into the mashed potatoes. But for a more dramatic presentation, you can divide the mashed potatoes among individual serving plates before adding the herb mixture; then, in the center of each mound of potatoes, make a small indentation and spoon in a small pool of the herb mixture.

SERVES 6 TO 8

3 pounds russet baking potatoes, peeled and cut into cubes
¾ cup half-and-half, warmed
4 tablespoons unsalted butter
Sea salt
White pepper
½ cup finely minced chives
½ cup chopped chervil

Cook the potatoes in boiling water until tender, about 25 minutes; drain.

In a medium saucepan, combine the potatoes, the half-and-half, 1 tablespoon of the butter, a generous pinch of salt, and a small pinch of white pepper. Using a masher with a grid or multi-holed mashing plate (for finer, lumpless mashing), mash and stir the potato mixture until smooth. Set aside.

In a small skillet, warm the remaining butter over medium-low heat, stirring frequently. Add the chives and chervil. Stir to coat with the butter. Then remove from heat. Now you can do one of two things: (1) add the herb-butter mixture, stir in with a wooden spoon, and serve; or (2) serve the mashed potatoes, then, in the center of each mound of potato make a little "pool" of herb-butter, about 1 tablespoon in each serving, leaving it in a pool or making a little S-shaped swirl.

eggplant, tomato, and zucchini gratin

THIS EASY BAKED VEGETABLE DISH, aromatic with thyme, basil, garlic, and onions, is an immutable part of summertime alfresco dinners in Provence. Every cook has his or her own version, but in general, they don't vary substantially from this one. I like to serve this with a leg of lamb cooked under the dome on the barbecue.

SERVES 6

Salt

2 pounds eggplant, cut into $\frac{1}{2}$-inch slices

3 tablespoons unsalted butter

5 tablespoons olive oil

2 medium onions, diced

2 cloves garlic, minced

2 pounds zucchini, cut into $\frac{1}{4}$-inch slices

2 pounds tomatoes, cut into $\frac{1}{4}$-inch slices

$\frac{1}{2}$ cup chopped basil

2 tablespoons thyme leaves, lightly crushed

3 tablespoons chopped parsley

Freshly ground black pepper

$\frac{1}{2}$ cup fine dry bread crumbs

$\frac{1}{4}$ cup freshly grated Parmigiano-Reggiano cheese

Bring a large saucepan of salted water to a boil. Add the eggplant slices, return to a boil, and cook for 5 minutes. Drain, place the slices on paper towels, pat the tops dry, and set aside.

Preheat the oven to 375° F. In a medium skillet, heat the butter and 3 tablespoons of the oil over medium heat. Add the onions and garlic and cook, stirring frequently, until the onions and garlic soften and begin to become translucent, about 4 minutes. Remove from the heat and set the pan aside.

In a greased 9- by 13-inch baking dish, or perhaps one a little larger, assemble the vegetables: starting at one end of the dish, arrange the eggplant in an overlapping row; repeat with the zucchini, slightly overlapping the eggplant, then with the tomatoes, slightly overlapping the zucchini. Repeat, filling the dish with alternating rows of the vegetables. Spread the onion mixture over the vegetables, then sprinkle on the basil, thyme, parsley, a pinch of salt, and several generous turns of the pepper mill. In a small bowl, combine the bread crumbs and the cheese, then sprinkle over the top of the vegetables. Drizzle the remaining 2 tablespoons oil over the bread crumb mixture, then bake in the center of the oven until the vegetables are tender and the top is thoroughly browned, about 25 minutes. Serve immediately.

fish and shellfish

pan-roasted arctic char
with thyme-syrah wine sauce

A FAVORITE RECIPE FROM THE VENERABLE HOTEL MONT CERVIN in the Swiss mountain resort of Zermatt, this is a light but richly flavored dish. The freshwater char fillets are served with a red wine reduction sauce smoothed with butter and scented with thyme. If the pink-fleshed arctic char is unavailable, substitute salmon.

SERVES 4

For the Sauce

1 cup Syrah or other dry red wine

1 tablespoon minced shallot

1 teaspoon thyme leaves, lightly crushed

¼ cup fish stock (or substitute 2 tablespoons
   clam juice and 2 tablespoons water)

¾ cup chicken stock

3 white peppercorns, crushed

4 tablespoons unsalted butter, chilled,
   cut into small pieces

Coarse salt

Freshly ground black pepper

For the Fish

Four 6-ounce skinless arctic char fillets

Coarse salt

Freshly ground black pepper

1 tablespoon peanut or other vegetable oil

1 tablespoon unsalted butter

Make the sauce: Place the wine, shallot, and thyme in a small saucepan and simmer over medium-high heat until reduced by half. Add the fish stock, chicken stock, and the white peppercorns and continue to simmer until reduced by two-thirds. Strain the reduction through a fine-mesh sieve and return it to the saucepan. Remove from the heat and set aside.

Make the fish: Season the fish with salt and pepper on both sides. Heat the oil and butter in a large skillet over medium-high heat. Add the fish and cook without disturbing until the edges begin to brown, 3 to 5 minutes. Turn the fish and continue cooking until it flakes easily, 3 to 5 minutes more. Arrange on warm serving plates.

Bring the wine mixture to a simmer over medium-low heat, then, whisking constantly, add the chilled butter one piece at a time. Adjust the seasoning with salt and pepper, spoon around the fish, and serve.

manila clams
with garlic and sweet marjoram

THIS RECIPE, CREATED BY CHARLENE ROLLINS, chef of New Sammy's Cowboy Bistro in Talent, Oregon, is a delectable variation of spaghetti with clam sauce. The recipe calls for serving the clam mixture over pasta, but Rollins suggests you could also serve the clams and broth in a bowl without pasta as a light first course. Of her composition of clams with butter, garlic, and sweet marjoram, Rollins says, "You must try it; it's one of those special affinities." Manila clams are a popular species of small Pacific Coast clam. In other parts of the country, substitute littlenecks.

SERVES 4

4 pounds Manila clams
4 tablespoons unsalted butter
4 tablespoons minced garlic
$\frac{1}{2}$ bunch sweet marjoram, leaves only
$\frac{1}{4}$ teaspoon hot red pepper flakes
$\frac{1}{2}$ cup dry white wine
1 pound angel-hair pasta or thin linguine or spaghetti
Freshly ground black pepper

Soak the clams in cold water to cover for about 30 minutes, to draw out any grit. If you're serving the clams with pasta, put a large pot of water on to boil.

In a medium sauté pan over low heat, melt the butter with the garlic, marjoram, and red pepper flakes. When the butter is just melted, stir in the wine and 1 cup water. Bring to a simmer and cook, covered, for about 8 minutes, adding water if necessary.

Lift the clams out of the soaking water, leaving the grit behind. Scrub thoroughly, discarding any clams that don't close up tightly, and any clams that are too heavy for their size.

Add the pasta to the pot of boiling water.

Raise the heat under the broth to high (you should have about $1\frac{1}{2}$ cups liquid). As soon as the broth comes to a boil, add the clams and cover the pan. Cook for 2 to 3 minutes, and as the clams open, immediately remove them to a bowl. Discard any that do not open after 5 minutes.

When the pasta is al dente, drain it and add it to the simmering broth, then use tongs to divide the pasta among 4 individual serving bowls. Return the clams to the broth to reheat briefly, then divide the clams among the serving bowls and pour the broth over. Season to taste with pepper and serve immediately.

center-cut cod fillets
with white beans and chanterelle
mushrooms in lemon-basil sauce

AT THE SERENE FRENCH-COUNTRY INN, the Hostellerie de L'Abbaye de la Celle, surrounded by lovely gardens and an old stone wall in the heart of Provence near the town of Brignoles, chef Benoît Witz's menu is inspired by products of the Mediterranean region. For this recipe, in which the fish is lightly salted with coarse salt to firm the texture, he uses a mild white-fleshed fish local to the Mediterranean Sea called mostelle. When this fish is unavailable, cod or seabass both work nicely with the savory white beans.

SERVES 4

4 center-cut cod fillets, about $\frac{1}{3}$ pound each, skin on

$\frac{1}{3}$ cup coarse sea salt

1 cup white beans, such as navy or Great Northern,
soaked overnight in water to cover, and drained

1 small onion, halved

1 carrot

1 sprig thyme

Fine sea salt

Freshly ground black pepper

6 tablespoons olive oil

$\frac{1}{2}$ pound fresh chanterelles or other wild mushrooms,
such as shiitakes, cleaned and trimmed

1 shallot, minced

4 baby zucchini, whole; or 1 medium zucchini, quartered

1 cup basil, loosely packed, finely julienned

Juice of 1 lemon

Place the cod fillets on a platter, skin side down. Sprinkle the coarse salt over the fillets, then set aside for 45 minutes. Rinse the fillets, pat dry, lightly cover with plastic wrap, and set in the refrigerator until ready to use.

Combine the beans, onion, carrot, and thyme in a large saucepan. Cover with cold water and bring to a boil over medium heat. Lower the heat to medium-low, cover, and cook until the beans are tender, about $1\frac{1}{2}$ hours. Drain, transfer to a bowl, add fine salt and pepper to taste, stir gently to combine, and set aside. In a large, clean casserole, warm 2 tablespoons of the oil over medium heat. Add the mushrooms and sauté, stirring frequently, until the mushrooms begin to give off their liquid, about 3 minutes. Pour off the juice and reserve. To the mushrooms add the shallot and zucchini, and cook, stirring frequently, until the shallots soften and the zucchini is tender, about 5 minutes. Add the beans and the reserved mushroom liquid and stir to combine. Lower the heat to medium-low, cover, and cook until the beans are heated through, about 8 minutes.

Meanwhile, in a medium skillet, heat 2 tablespoons of the oil over medium heat. Add the cod fillets, skin side down, lower the heat to medium-low, and cook for 7 to 8 minutes, until the fish is firm and cooked through; do not salt the fillets again. Remove the pan from the heat and set aside.

Add the basil and lemon juice to the bean mixture just before the end of its cooking time, then add the remaining oil and stir to bind the oil with the lemon juice and the cooking juices. Place the fillets on top of the bean mixture, cover the casserole, bring to the table, and serve immediately.

grilled striped bass with orzo, upland cress, and ginger-peach salsa

WIDELY REGARDED AS THE MOST BEAUTIFUL RESORT on the gracious and historic New England island of Nantucket, the Wauwinet occupies a vast property outside of town with frontage on both the Atlantic Ocean and Nantucket Bay. Here, bathed by sun, fog, and briny breezes, a large vegetable and herb garden flourishes under the care of Executive Chef Chris Freeman, who creates menus for Wauwinet's Toppers Restaurant. Freeman creates menus inspired by products fresh from his garden and fresh from the sea. In this innovative recipe, striped bass fillets are served on a bed of orzo and upland cress—a mild relative of watercress—and topped with a ginger- and basil-flavored peach salsa. If you don't grow upland cress in your garden, substitute watercress, reducing the amount to 4 cups and using only the topmost sprigs.

SERVES 6

For the Salsa

1 cup peeled and diced peaches (see note)
$\frac{1}{2}$ tablespoon finely diced red onion
1 tablespoon finely diced sweet red pepper
1 fresh cayenne pepper, minced
1 tablespoon minced garlic
1 tablespoon minced fresh ginger
1 tablespoon chopped basil
1 scallion, white and light green parts only, finely sliced on the bias
$1\frac{1}{2}$ tablespoons lime juice
$1\frac{1}{2}$ tablespoons rice wine vinegar
3 tablespoons extra-virgin olive oil
Salt
Freshly ground black pepper

For the Orzo

$\frac{1}{2}$ teaspoon saffron threads (optional)
Salt
2 cups orzo
Olive oil
2 large bunches upland cress, rinsed, large stems removed (about 6 cups), or 4 cups watercress, top sprigs only
Freshly ground black pepper

For the Bass

Six 6-ounce striped bass fillets, skin on
Olive oil
Salt
Freshly ground black pepper
Basil oil
Sprigs of basil for garnish

Make the salsa: Combine all the ingredients for the salsa in a bowl and set aside for 2 to 6 hours, to allow the flavors to develop.

Prepare a charcoal fire or preheat the broiler.

Cook the orzo: Bring 2 quarts water to a boil; add the saffron and ½ teaspoon salt. Add the orzo, stir and cook until al dente, 8 to 10 minutes.

Meanwhile, cook the bass: Lightly brush the fillets with olive oil, season with salt and pepper, and grill or broil until just cooked through and opaque in the center, about 4 minutes per side, depending on the thickness of the fillets and the heat of the charcoal.

Drain the orzo and toss with a touch of olive oil and the cress, then add salt and pepper to taste. Divide the orzo among 6 large serving plates, and set the bass fillets on top. Spoon some of the salsa over the fillets and use the remaining salsa to decorate the plate. Drizzle with a few drops of basil oil and garnish with sprigs of basil. Serve immediately.

NOTE: To peel peaches, blanch them for 30 seconds in boiling water, drain, transfer to a bowl of cold water, and slip off the skins.

salmon with dill, purple potatoes, spinach, roasted peppers, and dill gribiche sauce

IN THE TINY TOWN OF TALENT, OREGON, chef Charlene Rollins cooks up meals at her New Sammy's Cowboy Bistro that have brought her not only statewide but national attention. Everything she creates is sparklingly fresh and imaginative, using only organic produce. In this recipe, virtually any kind of filleted fish would work, Rollins notes. "It's the dill," she says, "that ties everything together into a tasty ensemble—a broth that marries the flavors of all the vegetables with a generous quantity of dill, and the dill (and dill pickles) in the gribiche sauce that melts into the fish and mixes with the broth." You'll have more than you'll need of the gribiche sauce—a variation of a traditional French mayonnaise-based sauce—but you can store it in the refrigerator for several weeks, and use it on sandwiches, cold meats or fish, even as a salad dressing.

SERVES 4

8 small purple potatoes, cut in half lengthwise

1 sweet red pepper, roasted and peeled,
   seeds removed

2 medium leeks, white and light green parts only

1 red onion

8 shiitake mushrooms, stems removed

2 tablespoons chopped dill

5 tablespoons butter

Salt

Four 6-ounce salmon fillets

Freshly ground black pepper

2 tablespoons olive oil

2 bunches spinach, stems removed, washed

$\frac{1}{2}$ cup Dill Gribiche Sauce (recipe follows)

Dill sprigs

Cook the potatoes in boiling water until just tender, 8 to 10 minutes. Drain and set aside. Cut the roasted pepper into 1-inch squares. Cut the leeks crosswise into $\frac{1}{4}$-inch rounds and wash thoroughly. Dice the onion. Wipe the mushrooms with a paper towel to remove any dirt, and cut the caps into quarters.

In a large sauté pan or saucepan, put the potatoes, roasted pepper, leeks, onion, mushrooms, chopped dill, butter, and 1 teaspoon salt. Pour in enough water to

just cover the vegetables and bring to a boil. Lower the heat to maintain a simmer; cook for 5 to 8 minutes, until the leeks and onion are soft.

Meanwhile, lightly season the salmon with salt and pepper on both sides. When the vegetables are almost done, heat the olive oil in a skillet over medium-high heat, and place the salmon in the skillet. Cook for 2 minutes, turn, and cook for 1 or 2 minutes longer, or to desired degree of doneness.

Add the spinach to the pan with the broth, and gently stir it in; cook for about 2 minutes, until the spinach is wilted and bright green.

Using a slotted spoon, transfer the vegetables from the broth to 4 individual serving plates; return the broth to the heat. Place the salmon over the vegetables. Pour a little of the broth over each portion. Spoon a line of gribiche sauce across the salmon and onto some of the vegetables. Season with salt and pepper, garnish with the dill sprigs, and serve immediately.

dill gribiche sauce

GRIBICHE, A MAYONNAISE-BASED SAUCE, is traditionally used on cold fish or meats. This recipe makes more than you need for the salmon, but it keeps well in the refrigerator. You can use this sauce as a spread on sandwiches or as a salad dressing (thinned with a bit more vinegar or pickle juice).

MAKES 2 CUPS

1 unshelled egg
1 tablespoon sherry vinegar
1 tablespoon pickle juice
$\frac{1}{4}$ teaspoon salt
1 packed cup parsley leaves
1 cup dill, with stems, coarsely chopped

$\frac{1}{3}$ cup capers
2 cups canola oil
4 shallots
3 medium-sized crunchy dill pickles
2 hard-boiled eggs, cooled and peeled

Bring a small pot of water to a boil. Gently place the egg in the boiling water, cover, and remove from the heat. Let stand for 6 minutes, then remove the egg and crack it into the bowl of a food processor. Add the vinegar, pickle juice, and salt; process for 5 minutes. Add the parsley and dill and process for 5 minutes. Add the capers; then, with the processor running, gradually add the oil in a thin stream, until the mixture is thick but still pourable. If it's too thick, stir in a dash of pickle juice. Transfer the sauce to a sealable plastic container.

Finely mince the shallots, and dice the pickles and hard-boiled eggs; stir them into the sauce and season to taste with pickle juice or vinegar. The gribiche will keep for a week or two in the refrigerator.

quick salmon soup
with chopped herbs

IN HER HOME IN THE FRENCH COUNTRYSIDE just south of the Loire Valley, painter and fine cook Aude Kamlet prepares simple, delicious meals using the abundance of herbs from her *potager*, or kitchen garden, just outside. This easy salmon recipe is a quick soup that Kamlet serves as a meal for two with fresh, crusty bread, a green salad, and the lovely dry white wine from Touraine. The whole meal is ready within half an hour.

SERVES 2

3 tablespoons canola oil, or other light oil

1 medium onion, chopped

2 tablespoons flour

3 cups chicken stock

$\frac{1}{4}$ cup finely chopped parsley

$\frac{1}{4}$ cup finely chopped watercress, tops only

$\frac{1}{4}$ cup mix of some or all of these finely chopped herbs:

dill, basil, tarragon, cilantro

Salt

Freshly ground black pepper

Two 6-ounce boneless salmon steaks

1 tablespoon capers, drained

In a deep skillet or a medium sauté pan, heat the oil over medium heat. Add the onion and cook, stirring frequently, until it is soft and slightly golden, about 4 minutes. Add the flour and stir to blend, then add the stock and stir until the mixture thickens slightly, about 3 minutes. Add the parsley, watercress, and herb mixture and stir to combine. Season to taste with salt and pepper. Add the salmon steaks, cover, and cook until the fish is flaky, about 10 minutes. Stir in the capers, then remove from heat. Using a slotted spatula, transfer each salmon steak to a large, warmed soup bowl. Divide the broth among the two bowls and serve immediately.

fillet of sea bream
with potato scales, zucchini confit, and warm vinaigrette

THIS ATTRACTIVELY PRESENTED DISH was created by chef Jerôme Fessard for guests in the private dining room of the stylish Hotel Lancaster, just off Paris's Champs-Elysées. A medley of herbs enhances the composition: thyme, bay leaves, and garlic flavor the zucchini accompaniment, while wild thyme, chervil, and savory enhance the warm tomato vinaigrette. Use regular thyme if the wild variety is not available. The recipe was created with a fish the French call *daurade royale*, or sea bream, a fish in the porgy family difficult to find in the United States. If sea bream is not available, use snapper or sea bass fillets.

SERVES 2

¼ cup unsalted butter

1 pound white potatoes

Two 8-ounce skinless sea bream fillets

½ pound zucchini

¾ cup olive oil

1 sprig thyme, bottom of stem removed

2 bay leaves

2 cloves garlic, blanched

Salt

4 tablespoons sherry vinegar

1 sprig wild thyme, bottom of stem removed

1 sprig savory, leaves only

1 sprig chervil, leaves only

2 small tomatoes, peeled, seeded, and diced

Freshly ground black pepper

Sprigs of herbs for garnish

Melt the butter. Peel the potatoes, slice into paper-thin rounds, and put in the butter to coat the slices thoroughly. Place the sea bream fillets on two plates. Remove the potato slices from the butter and arrange over the fillets to resemble scales; brush with a bit of the melted butter. Place the fillets in the refrigerator to allow the butter to firm up.

Cut the zucchini lengthwise into ½-inch slices. Heat ¼ cup of the oil in a small skillet over medium-high heat, add the zucchini, and cook undisturbed until the slices are thoroughly browned on one side, about 5 minutes. Add the thyme, bay leaves, garlic cloves, and salt to taste; stir gently to combine. Lower the heat to low and cook until the zucchini is caramelized, very soft, and browned, about 10 minutes longer.

Meanwhile, in a small saucepan bring the vinegar to a boil; cook for 3 minutes, remove from the heat, and add the remaining oil, the wild thyme, savory, chervil, tomatoes, salt, and pepper to taste. Cover and set aside.

Heat 3 tablespoons of the melted butter in a large nonstick sauté pan over medium-high heat. Using a large spatula, carefully transfer the potato-topped fillets to the pan, potato side down, and cook undisturbed for 8 to 10 minutes, until the potatoes are browned and crisp. Preheat the broiler. Season the fillets with salt and pepper and place the pan under the broiler until the fish is just cooked through, about 2 minutes.

Use tongs to arrange the zucchini confit in a star pattern on individual serving plates, place the fish over, potato side up, and garnish with sprigs of herbs. Serve with the warm vinaigrette in a sauceboat on the side.

kumamoto oysters
with opal basil gelée

IN THIS RECIPE FROM ROCCO DISPIRITO, the brilliant young chef of the Union Pacific restaurant in Manhattan, oysters on the half-shell are garnished with tiny cubes of tangy, burgundy-red gelée flavored with two basils, shallots, and red-wine vinegar. The gelée is an imaginative variation of a classic *vinaigre à l'echalote*—a shallot vinegar—often served in France with a platter of fresh oysters and other shellfish. If you cannot find the small Kumamoto oysters that DiSpirito serves at Union Pacific, use whatever variety you find that are freshest and most appealing. If Thai basil is unavailable, use regular basil with the addition of two small sprigs of mint.

SERVES 8

6 cups red wine vinegar
$\frac{1}{4}$ pound chopped opal basil
$\frac{1}{4}$ pound chopped Thai basil
$\frac{1}{2}$ cup chopped shallots
$\frac{1}{4}$ cup black peppercorns, cracked
1 tablespoon sugar
Three $\frac{1}{4}$-ounce packets unflavored gelatin
32 Kumamoto oysters (or other small, fresh oysters), shucked, on the
half-shell with their liquid

In a large saucepan over medium heat, combine the vinegar, basils, shallots, peppercorns, and sugar. Bring just to a simmer, remove from the heat, cover, and set aside to steep for 2 hours. Strain the liquid through a fine-mesh sieve lined with several layers of rinsed and squeezed cheesecloth and discard the solids; the liquid should be clear. Put $\frac{1}{2}$ cup cold water in a medium mixing bowl and sprinkle the gelatin over; let stand for 1 minute.

Prepare an ice-water bath in the sink or in a large bowl. Reheat the vinegar mixture over low heat until it comes to a simmer. Pour it over the softened gelatin and whisk to combine. Place the bowl in the ice-water bath and whisk often to cool the mixture, until the mixture is slightly viscous but not set, about 15 minutes. Pour the gelatin mixture into two 11- by 15-inch baking sheets to a depth of about $\frac{1}{4}$ inch. Refrigerate until the gelée has set, about 45 minutes.

Arrange the oysters flat on a serving platter. Cut the gelée into tiny cubes and sprinkle over the oysters, or cut it into larger pieces and lay one piece over each oyster to cover. Serve immediately.

seared sea scallops
with lavender, lime, and champagne

IT IS INDEED SPA CUISINE, but the dishes prepared by Executive Chef Sue Chapman at California's The Lodge at Skylonda soar far beyond the general perception of healthful, low-calorie fare as nourishing but unexciting. Bland and boring this cuisine is not. In her imaginative recipes, Chapman creates elegant, colorful, flavor-saturated food that pleases the Lodge's discriminating West Coast diners, whether they're dieting or not. This dazzling scallop dish, combining shallots, garlic, lime, and lavender in a rich, flavorful champagne sauce, has only 203 calories per serving.

SERVES 6

Cooking spray
2 pounds large sea scallops
1 teaspoon chopped garlic
1 tablespoon minced shallots
1 cup champagne
Juice of 2 limes
1 teaspoon grated or minced lime zest
1 tablespoon unsalted butter
1 teaspoon fresh lavender flowers
1 small bunch chives, sliced on the bias into 1-inch pieces
1 teaspoon pink peppercorns

In a large skillet coated with cooking spray, sear the scallops on both sides over medium-high heat, then transfer to a large plate, cover loosely with aluminum foil, and keep warm in a very low oven. Return the skillet to medium heat, add the garlic and the shallots, then stir in the champagne and deglaze the pan, scraping up any browned bits on the bottom of the pan. Add the lime juice and lime zest and cook until the liquid is reduced by half. Add the butter and cook until melted, stirring constantly. Add the lavender flowers and whisk the sauce until it emulsifies. Remove from the heat. Arrange the scallops on warmed serving plates, pour the sauce over, garnish with the chives and pink peppercorns, and serve immediately.

mushroom and tarragon
stuffed sole with hollandaise sauce

TALENTED NEW ENGLAND CHEF BARBARA FENNER grew up on the island of Martha's Vineyard, where she has headed up the kitchens of several top restaurants. Now she has her own enterprise, the beloved Menemsha Galley, founded more than forty years ago in the heart of the picturesque fishing village of Menemsha. This recipe is one of many seafood dishes inspired by the fish and shellfish that the local fishing boats bring in daily to the Menemsha docks.

SERVES 4

For the Fish

7 tablespoons unsalted butter

½ cup finely chopped onion

3 cups sliced mushrooms

3 tablespoons chopped tarragon

¾ cup dry white wine

2 cups plain bread crumbs

Salt

Freshly ground black pepper

Eight 2- to 3-ounce sole fillets or four 4- to
   6-ounce sole fillets

For the Hollandaise Sauce

3 egg yolks

½ cup unsalted butter, melted

1 tablespoon freshly squeezed lemon juice

Salt

White pepper

Cayenne pepper (optional)

Make the fish: In a large skillet, melt 4 tablespoons of the butter over medium heat. Add the onion and mushrooms and cook, stirring frequently, until the onions soften and the mushrooms begin to give off their liquid, about 4 minutes. Add the tarragon and wine, and bring the mixture to a boil over high heat. Cook, stirring frequently, until the liquid is slightly reduced, about 2 minutes. Remove from the heat and set aside to cool. Add the bread crumbs, stir to combine, then sea-

son to taste with salt and pepper.

Preheat the oven to 350° F. Pat any moisture off the sole fillets with paper towels. Divide the mushroom stuffing among the fillets, placing a portion in the center of each. Fold the two ends of the fillet over the center, snugly enclosing the filling. Place fillet packets seam side down in a baking pan large enough to hold them. Melt the remaining butter in the microwave or in a small saucepan, then drizzle over the top of the fish.

Bake until the fish is firm to the touch, and the stuffing is heated through, 25 to 30 minutes.

Meanwhile, prepare the hollandaise sauce: In the top of a double boiler, or in a bowl set over about 2 inches of simmering water, combine the egg yolks and 1½ tablespoons cold water. Whisk the yolks until they are slightly thickened. Gradually whisk in the butter and cook the mixture until smooth and satiny. If the sauce becomes too thick, stir in a tablespoon or so of water. Remove from the heat and season with the lemon juice, salt and white pepper to taste, and a tiny pinch of cayenne pepper if you wish. Transfer to a warmed sauceboat and serve immediately with the baked stuffed sole.

crispy crab dumplings
with chervil

THESE IRRESISTIBLE CRAB DUMPLINGS ARE A SPECIALTY at Aquarelle, the luminous restaurant of the Swissôtel-The Watergate in Washington, D.C. Aquarelle's acclaimed chef, Tim Barger, created these dumplings, flecked with chervil, to serve in a creamy corn soup, but they are also delicious as hors d'oeuvres or appetizers.

SERVES 4 AS AN APPETIZER, 8 AS HORS D'OEUVRES

8 sprigs chervil, minced
¼ cup white cornmeal
1 egg, lightly beaten
½ teaspoon sugar
½ teaspoon coarse salt

1 tablespoon heavy cream
½ cup lump crabmeat
Vegetable oil for frying
3 tablespoons hazelnut oil

Place half of the chervil in a medium bowl. Add the cornmeal, egg, sugar, and salt and stir to combine thoroughly. Add the cream, then gently fold in the crabmeat.

In a medium skillet, heat 2 inches vegetable oil and the hazelnut oil over medium-high heat. Mold the crabmeat mixture into tablespoon-size dumplings, then carefully drop them into the oil in batches; fry until crisp on all sides, about 2 minutes per batch. Transfer to a plate lined with a double layer of paper towels. Serve on a platter as an hors d'oeuvre or divided among 4 individual plates as an appetizer, garnished with remaining chervil.

meats and poultry

boeuf gardian
provençal beef stew

THIS SPICY AND VERY AROMATIC BEEF STEW is a traditional Provençal dish that originated with the cow-boys—*gardians*—of the wild and beautiful Camargue region of Provence. While the gardians usually prepared this dish using the meat of local bulls, which they herded, this adaptation features beef. It is traditionally accompanied by white rice. You can prepare it a day ahead and refrigerate until ready to serve; it only gets better with waiting.

SERVES 4 TO 6

3 tablespoons olive oil

2 medium onions, peeled and quartered

2 carrots, sliced into 1/4-inch rounds

2 pounds beef, round of chuck,
    cut into bite-size cubes

6 whole cloves garlic

1/2 cup minced Italian parsley

1 bay leaf

1 teaspoon chopped thyme

2 tomatoes, coarsely chopped

2 shallots, coarsely chopped

2 whole sprigs Italian parsley

1 celery stalk with leaves, coarsely chopped

One 750 ml bottle dry red wine,
    preferably Côtes du Rhône

1 medium onion studded with 4 cloves

1 strip orange rind, about 2 inches long
    and 1 inch wide

Pinch of ground cinnamon

1 teaspoon salt

1/4 teaspoon black peppercorns

Freshly ground black pepper

In a large skillet, heat the oil over medium heat. Add the quartered onions, the carrots, beef, garlic, minced parsley, bay leaf, and thyme and stir to combine. Cook, stirring frequently, until the onions and meat are very lightly browned, about 5 minutes. Add the tomatoes, shallots, parsley sprigs, and celery and stir to combine. Continue cooking until the meat is fully browned, then add the wine, clove-studded onion, orange rind, cinnamon, salt, and peppercorns and stir to combine. Cover the casserole, lower the heat to medium-low, and simmer for 3 to 4 hours, until the meat is very tender and the sauce has reduced by about half. Season to taste with pepper and serve immediately, accompanied with white rice.

chicken vindaye
with watercress salad

ORIGINALLY AN INDIAN DISH, chicken vindaye is now part of the traditional cuisine on the romantic island of Mauritius in the Indian Ocean. Mildly spicy and a little sweet, the vindaye is a delicious, versatile recipe you can also make with fish, prawns, or pork. This recipe comes from Nalam Nastili, Executive Chef of the island's Le Touessrok Hotel and Ile aux Cerfs. The slightly bitter flavor of the watercress contrasts nicely with the flavor of the vindaye chicken. Serve it with rice or warm bread.

SERVES 4

$\frac{1}{4}$ cup vegetable oil

$1\frac{1}{2}$ pounds boneless, skinless chicken breast, cut into bite-size cubes, blotted dry

1 large onion, peeled and cut lengthwise into 8 equal sections

1 tablespoon minced garlic

1 tablespoon powdered turmeric

$\frac{1}{4}$ cup red or white wine vinegar

$\frac{3}{4}$ cup chicken stock

1 teaspoon coarse-grained mustard such as Pomméry

Salt

Freshly ground black pepper

Red pepper flakes

2 bunches watercress, coarse stems removed

2 to 3 tablespoons olive oil

1 to 2 tablespoons freshly squeezed lemon juice

$\frac{1}{4}$ teaspoon maple syrup

4 sprigs cilantro

In a large, heavy skillet, heat about half of the vegetable oil over medium-high heat. Add the chicken and quickly brown on all sides, then remove with a slotted spoon to a bowl and set aside.

Add the remaining vegetable oil, stir in the onion and garlic, and cook until the onion just begins to color, stirring often, about 4 minutes. Stir in the turmeric and vinegar and cook until the liquid has almost evaporated, scraping up any browned bits on the bottom of the pan. Pour in the stock, add the mustard, and bring to a boil. Season to taste with salt, pepper, and red pepper flakes. Return the chicken to the pan and simmer until it is cooked through, about 5 minutes; set aside.

In a large bowl, toss the watercress with enough olive oil to coat the leaves. Season with salt and pepper. Add just enough lemon juice to balance the taste, then add the maple syrup and toss to combine thoroughly. Divide the watercress among 4 large serving plates. Spoon on the chicken, garnish with the cilantro, and serve.

roast cornish hens
with tarragon

ONE OF MY FAVORITE PARIS BISTROS IS D'CHEZ EUX, a warm and welcoming restaurant just across the street from the commanding UNESCO building in the heart of the 7th arrondissement. Here Jean-Pierre Court, continuing the family tradition established by his father, Albert, who acquired the restaurant, formerly a taxi-drivers' café, in 1963, greets every customer like a friend. The menu is full of beloved classics that the regular customers insist upon, among them cassoulet, fricassée of chicken with a morel-mushroom sauce, and this delicious dish, in which tender roast Cornish hens, stuffed with tarragon, are bathed in a tarragon-cream sauce. Serve it with green vegetables and a mixture of white and wild rice.

SERVES 4

Four 1-pound Cornish hens
4 tablespoons unsalted butter, softened
Salt
Freshly ground black pepper
2 bunches tarragon
$\frac{1}{2}$ cup Noilly Prat or other dry white vermouth
1 cup crème fraîche
3 tablespoons minced tarragon
$\frac{1}{2}$ cup chicken stock

Preheat the oven to 400° F. Rinse the hens inside and out with cold water and pat dry. Rub the hens all over with the butter, and put a pat of butter inside each. Season the hens with salt and pepper and stuff each with half a bunch of tarragon. Place in a roasting pan, breast side up, and roast for about 30 minutes, turning the pan from time to time, until the birds are evenly browned and the juices run clear when the thigh is pierced with a fork.

Remove the pan from the oven and spoon off and discard the fat, leaving the hens and a few tablespoons of the juices in the pan. Place over high heat. Add the vermouth and deglaze the pan, scraping up any browned bits on the bottom of the pan and spooning the juices over the hens. Transfer the hens to a platter and cover with tented foil to keep warm.

Put the roasting pan over medium heat, add the crème fraîche and the minced tarragon, and stir to combine. Add the stock and bring to a boil; cook for about 5 minutes, until the liquid has thickened to a sauce consistency. Add salt and pepper to taste.

Cut the hens in half through the breastbone and backbone. Place two halves on 4 individual serving plates and spoon the sauce over. Serve immediately.

herb-roasted chicken

IN THIS SAVORY, SUCCULENT ROAST CHICKEN, a mélange of aromatic herbs permeates the meat from both outside and in. You press an herb-butter blend in the pocket between the skin and the flesh, and you also stuff the cavity with rosemary and herb stems reserved during the preparation of the herb butter. The wonderful aroma that emanates from the kitchen as this chicken roasts will have hungry family and friends counting the minutes until dinnertime.

SERVES 4

One 4- to 5-pound roaster chicken
$\frac{1}{2}$ cup unsalted butter at room temperature
1 shallot, minced
2 tablespoons chopped chives
2 tablespoons chopped parsley, leaves only; stems reserved
2 tablespoons chopped chervil, leaves only; stems reserved
1 tablespoon chopped mint, leaves only; stems reserved
1 tablespoon chopped oregano, leaves only; stems reserved
2 teaspoons chopped tarragon, leaves only; stems reserved
2 teaspoons chopped thyme, leaves only; stems reserved
1 teaspoon finely julienned sage
Coarse salt
Freshly ground black pepper
2 large sprigs rosemary
1 small lemon, quartered
2 tablespoons olive oil
1 cup chicken stock
$\frac{1}{4}$ cup dry white vermouth, or dry white wine

Preheat the oven to 425° F. Rinse the chicken inside and out with cold water, pat dry, and set aside. In a small mixing bowl, combine the butter with the shallot, chives, parsley, chervil, mint, oregano, tarragon, thyme, sage, ½ teaspoon salt, and 5 or 6 turns of freshly ground pepper. Using the back of a fork, mash the ingredients together until blended.

Using your fingers, separate the skin of the chicken from the flesh, creating pockets above the thighs, on the back, above the wings, and over the neck. Continuing to use your fingers, take 1 to 2 tablespoons of the butter mixture and spread it, pressing firmly, under the skin and onto the flesh over the entire bird, using all but 1 tablespoon of the butter mixture. Season the cavity of the chicken with salt and pepper, then stuff with the remaining tablespoon of the butter mixture, the rosemary, lemon, and the reserved herb stems. Rub the oil all over the skin of the chicken, then season with salt and pepper.

Place the chicken in a roasting pan, set it in the center of the oven, and bake for 30 minutes. Baste with ½ cup of the stock, lower the heat to 350° F, and roast for 45 minutes to 1 hour longer, basting every 15 minutes or so, until the juices run clear when the thigh is pierced with a fork. Transfer the chicken to a wire rack placed on a platter, and set aside.

Place the roasting pan over high heat, add the vermouth and deglaze the pan, scraping up the browned bits on the bottom of the pan. Add the remaining stock, lower the heat to medium, and cook, stirring frequently, until the liquid is reduced by half. Remove from the heat, add the accumulated juices from the platter under the chicken, stir to blend, adjust the seasoning, then strain into a sauce boat. Carve the chicken and arrange on warmed serving plates, giving each person a portion with some herbs on the meat; or bring the bird to the table and carve there. Serve the sauce on the side.

herbed roast veal
with wild mushroom brioche bread pudding

CHEF JAMES STAIANO OF the Istana Restaurant at Manhattan's New York Palace Hotel makes this succulent, herb-infused veal roast for a glamorous New Year's Eve dinner. It is accompanied by a brioche bread pudding studded with wild mushrooms and a richly flavored Madeira wine sauce. If you have a friendly butcher, you might ask him to prepare the veal for you through the first step, below, providing him with the specified herbs, shallots, and olive oil.

SERVES 6 TO 8

For the Veal

1 tablespoon minced rosemary

1 tablespoon minced thyme

2 teaspoons chopped chervil

3 medium minced shallots

$\frac{1}{2}$ cup plus 2 tablespoons olive oil

4- to 4$\frac{1}{2}$-pound veal loin roast, thoroughly
 trimmed, butterflied to a thickness of
 $\frac{1}{4}$ to $\frac{1}{2}$ inch

Salt

Freshly ground white pepper

For the Brioche Bread Pudding

3 tablespoons unsalted butter, plus additional
 for the soufflé dish

2 medium shallots, minced

2$\frac{1}{2}$ cups sliced fresh wild mushrooms such as
 cremini, shiitakes, chanterelles, or a mixture

1 pint heavy cream

3 eggs, beaten

8 cups brioche bread, or challah bread,
 crusts removed, cut into 1$\frac{1}{4}$-inch cubes

Salt

Freshly ground black pepper

For the Madeira Sauce

1 tablespoon unsalted butter

2 medium shallots, chopped

1 cup medium Madeira

1 sprig thyme

1 bay leaf

4 black peppercorns, cracked

2 cups full-flavored veal demi-glace,
 or $\frac{1}{4}$ cup concentrated beef stock diluted
 in 2 cups warm water

120

Make the veal: At least 8 hours before serving, rub the herbs, shallots, and $\frac{1}{2}$ cup of the oil into both sides of the meat. Season with salt and pepper, then roll the veal up jelly-roll style, and tie it with butcher's string, cover lightly with plastic wrap, and refrigerate for about 8 hours.

Preheat the oven to 375° F. Heat an oven-proof skillet large enough to hold the meat over high heat. Add the remaining oil to the pan and brown the meat on all sides. Transfer the pan to the oven and roast until the meat is medium-rare, 38 to 45 minutes. (Meanwhile, prepare the brioche pudding.) Take the meat out of the oven and let it rest for 10 minutes. Remove the strings and cut the meat crosswise into $\frac{1}{2}$-inch-thick slices. Serve accompanied by the Madeira sauce and the brioche pudding.

Make the brioche bread pudding: Butter an 8-cup (large) soufflé or baking dish. Heat 3 tablespoons butter in a large skillet over medium-high heat. Add the shallots and sauté until translucent, 1 to 2 minutes.

Stir in the mushrooms and cook until just softened. Remove from the heat.

Combine the cream and eggs, then pour the mixture over the mushrooms, scraping up any browned bits on the bottom of the pan. Put the brioche in a large bowl and pour the mushroom mixture over, turning gently to mix. Season generously with salt and pepper. Transfer to a baking dish and bake alongside the roasting veal until puffy and golden brown, about 30 minutes. Remove the pudding from the oven and let it rest for 5 minutes before serving.

Make the Madeira sauce: While the pudding is cooking, heat the butter in a small saucepan over medium heat. Add the shallots and sweat until tender. Add the Madeira, thyme, bay leaf, and peppercorns. Bring the mixture to a boil and cook until the liquid has almost completely evaporated. Stir in the demi-glace and simmer for 10 minutes. Strain through a fine-mesh sieve, taste for seasonings, and serve in a sauceboat.

tangerine and thyme-scented roast turkey

SCENTED WITH THYME AND STUFFED WITH LEMON and tangerine, this is a wonderfully aromatic Caribbean-inspired Thanksgiving turkey from Todd Weisz, Executive Chef of the Turnberry Isle Resort and Club in Aventura, Florida.

SERVES 8 TO 10

For the Turkey

1 tangerine, or navel orange, washed and patted dry

1 lemon, washed and patted dry

½ cup unsalted butter, softened

12- to 14-pound fresh whole turkey

1 tablespoon salt

2 teaspoons freshly ground black pepper

1 bunch thyme

1 bunch sage

1 bulb garlic, halved crosswise

For the Gravy

Reserved juices from the turkey roasting pan

1 cup dry white wine

6 tablespoons flour

2 cups turkey stock, or chicken stock

1 tablespoon chopped thyme

1 tablespoon chopped sage

Salt

Freshly ground black pepper

1 tablespoon unsalted butter

To make the turkey: Preheat the oven to 425° F. Grate the zest from the tangerine and the lemon; quarter the tangerine and the lemon and set aside. Rub the butter all over the turkey and put a pat or two inside the cavity. Season the turkey inside and out with the tangerine and lemon zest, salt, and pepper. Pack the cavity with the quartered tangerine and lemon, the thyme, sage, and garlic, then truss the turkey. Place the turkey on a rack in a roasting pan breast side up, and roast in the center of the oven for 30 minutes. Lower the temperature to 325° F and cook for about 3 hours,

or until a meat thermometer inserted in the fleshy part of the thigh registers 180° F and the juices run clear when the thigh is pierced with a skewer.

When the turkey turns golden brown, about halfway through its roasting time, cover with aluminum foil and add 1 cup water. Turn the roasting pan as it bakes so that the turkey browns evenly, and baste every 20 minutes or so. Transfer the turkey to a serving platter, reserving the juices in the roasting pan; cover the turkey loosely with foil. Let it rest for about 20 minutes, then bring to the table and serve with the gravy.

To make the gravy: Skim all the fat from the pan juices, reserving ⅓ cup fat. Place the roasting pan over medium heat, add the wine, and bring to a boil, deglazing the pan and scraping up any browned bits on the bottom of the pan. Lower the heat to medium-low and simmer until the wine is reduced by half, about 5 minutes.

Meanwhile, in a small saucepan, combine the reserved fat and the flour. Cook the mixture over medium heat, whisking constantly, for 3 to 4 minutes, until you notice a nutty aroma. This is the roux, which is used to thicken the gravy. Add the turkey stock and the reduced wine mixture to the roux in a steady stream, whisking constantly as you pour. Bring to a boil over medium-high heat, then lower the heat to medium-low and simmer, stirring occasionally, for 10 to 15 minutes. Strain through a fine-mesh sieve into a clean saucepan, add the thyme, sage, salt, and pepper to taste, and stir to combine. Keep warm until ready to serve. Just before serving, whisk in the butter, transfer to a warmed gravy boat, and bring it to the table with the turkey.

sirloin steak and orange kabobs

IN THIS CHANGE-OF-PACE beef kabob recipe, the steak marinates in a pungent sauce flavored with thyme. If you have any dried sprigs of thyme saved, throw them on the coals just before removing the kabobs to enhance the beef with a whisper of smoky fragrance from the thyme. Serve with a rice pilaf and perhaps a radicchio, endive, and watercress salad.

SERVES 6

$3/4$ cup fresh orange juice

2 cloves garlic, minced

4 tablespoons olive oil

3 tablespoons thyme leaves, lightly crushed

1 tablespoon Dijon mustard

1 tablespoon soy sauce

$1/4$ teaspoon salt

1 teaspoon freshly ground black pepper

2 pounds boneless sirloin, sliced diagonally across the grain into $1/4$-inch strips

4 navel oranges, peeled and cut into $1/4$-inch rounds, then each slice quartered

3 navel oranges, cut into wedges

6 sprigs thyme

In a medium glass or ceramic bowl, combine the orange juice, garlic, oil, thyme leaves, mustard, soy sauce, salt, and pepper, and stir to combine. Add the sliced steak and stir to coat the pieces with the marinade. Cover with plastic wrap and set aside to marinate for 45 minutes.

Prepare a charcoal fire.

Weave the steak onto 6 skewers, ribbon-candy style. As you thread the strips onto the skewers, place a slice of orange between each loop of steak. Grill over medium-hot coals, basting frequently with the marinade, to desired doneness, about 10 minutes for medium-rare. Serve immediately on a platter garnished with orange wedges and sprigs of thyme.

herbed beef pie
with potato-corn crust

THIS SAVORY PIE, A CROSS BETWEEN *HACHIS PARMENTIER*—a French shepherd's pie—and a South American beef pie, was born one evening when I thought I had ample ingredients for both but discovered I didn't have sufficient ingredients for either. It was a serendipitous composition, aromatic with sage, oregano, and thyme, and succulent with the addition of golden raisins and chopped green olives, ingredients sometimes found in the Argentinean empanada. You could make this dish spicier—the way my husband, Steve, likes it—by adding 1 small diced red pepper with the onions, and 1 teaspoon ground cinnamon, 1 teaspoon ground cumin, and ½ teaspoon red pepper flakes stirred in with the tomatoes, olives, and raisins. A lusty Spanish Rioja wine accompanies this dish beautifully.

SERVES 4 TO 6

For the Crust

2 pounds potatoes, peeled and cubed

4 tablespoons unsalted butter

⅓ cup whole milk, warmed

Salt

Freshly ground black pepper

Freshly grated nutmeg

½ cup corn kernels

3 tablespoons minced parsley

For the Filling

¼ pound bacon, coarsely chopped

1½ pounds lean ground beef, such as sirloin

1 clove garlic, crushed and chopped

1 medium onion, chopped

¼ cup chopped parsley

1 teaspoon chopped oregano

1 teaspoon thyme leaves, lightly crushed

3 sage leaves, finely chopped

3 tablespoons dry white vermouth or
   dry white wine

1 cup ripe tomatoes, peeled, seeded, and chopped
   or crushed canned tomatoes

⅓ cup pitted and chopped green olives

¼ cup golden raisins

Salt

Freshly ground black pepper

Make the crust: In a large saucepan, combine the potatoes with enough water to generously cover, and bring to a boil. Cook for 7 to 10 minutes, until the potatoes are tender. Drain, transfer to a mixing bowl, and mash to a fine puree with the butter, milk, and salt, pepper, and nutmeg to taste. Add the corn and parsley and stir to combine. Adjust the seasoning, then cover with plastic wrap and set aside.

Make the filling: Preheat the oven to 375° F. In a large skillet, brown the bacon lightly over medium heat. Add the beef, stir to combine and break up any large chunks, and cook, stirring frequently, until the beef has lost all its pinkness, but hasn't yet started to brown. Add the garlic, onion, parsley, oregano, thyme, sage, and vermouth, and stir to combine. Cook, stirring frequently, until the onions begin to soften, about 10 minutes. Add the tomatoes, olives, raisins, salt, and pepper to taste, and stir to combine. Cook, stirring fre-

quently, for about 5 minutes, until the mixture begins to bubble, then lower the heat to low and simmer for 5 minutes. Remove from the heat and transfer the mixture to a buttered baking dish, such as a 2-quart casserole or soufflé dish. Smooth the top of the mixture, then spoon on the potato mixture and gently spread it evenly over the top. Bake in the center of the oven for about 40 minutes, until the top is golden brown. Remove from the oven, let cool slightly for 5 minutes, then serve.

rosemary-thyme grilled chicken
breasts with herb butter

THIS AROMATIC AND SUCCULENT BARBECUED CHICKEN gets its flavor from herbs rubbed on the skin before grilling, and from the herb butter, which melts over the top as you serve it. Serve with rice or a rice salad and a green vegetable such as asparagus or green beans. If you have any herb butter left over, wrap it in plastic wrap and freeze it to use later on steak or grilled fish.

SERVES 6

For the Herb Butter
1 shallot, minced
$\frac{1}{2}$ cup unsalted butter, softened
2 tablespoons minced rosemary
2 tablespoons minced thyme
2 tablespoons freshly squeezed lemon juice
$\frac{1}{4}$ teaspoon salt
$\frac{1}{4}$ teaspoon freshly ground black pepper

For the Chicken
2 tablespoons minced rosemary
2 tablespoons minced thyme
1 teaspoon coarse sea salt
$\frac{1}{2}$ teaspoon freshly ground black pepper
2 tablespoons olive oil
3 large boneless chicken breasts ($\frac{3}{4}$ to 1 pound each), ideally with the skin on, halved

Make the herb butter: In a small bowl, cream together all the ingredients. Cover with plastic wrap and refrigerate at least half an hour to firm up and to let the herbs flavor the butter. (You can make the herb butter several hours ahead.) Remove from the refrigerator a few minutes before you're ready to use it.

Make the chicken: In a small bowl, combine the rosemary, thyme, salt, and pepper, then spread the mixture over the surface of a large plate. Rub the chicken all over with the olive oil, then press each piece onto the herb mixture so that both sides are thoroughly coated. Cook over medium coals, turning once, until the chicken is cooked through, 10 to 15 minutes total. Remove to individual serving plates, place about 1 tablespoon of the herb butter on the top of each piece, and serve immediately.

lamb croustillant with herbs

IN THIS SPECIAL-OCCASION SPRINGTIME recipe from René Bérard, chef and owner of Provence's Hostellerie Bérard in La Cadière d'Azur, the flavor of a succulent rack of lamb is enhanced by a delicious, buttery herb crust flecked with basil and thyme. The laying on of the crust and the cooking require a bit of finesse—mainly in turning the lamb in the skillet so that the crust stays on—but all you really need is patience and two spatulas, one on the top of the piece of lamb, one on the bottom. To expedite the preparation, you can have your butcher prepare the lamb through the first step.

SERVES 4

One 7- to 8-pound rack of lamb (have the butcher split it into 2 halves)
Salt
Freshly ground black pepper
2 pounds fresh fava beans in shells, or 1 pound dried shelled fava beans
1 bunch young carrots with tops
8 white baby onions with tops, or 16 pearl onions
1 sprig basil, washed, stems removed
2 cups fresh bread crumbs
1 egg yolk
$\frac{1}{2}$ cup plus 2 tablespoons unsalted butter, softened
$1\frac{1}{4}$ cups full-flavored lamb stock (see note) or beef stock
2 sprigs thyme
Salt
White pepper
Red pepper flakes (optional)

Bone the rack of lamb, reserving the bones and meat trimmings; trim and discard the fat. Cut the loin into 4 equal pieces, season lightly with salt and pepper, and set aside in the refrigerator.

Wash and shell the fresh fava beans. Blanch in boiling salted water for 3 minutes, drain, and plunge into cold water, slipping off the tough skins; drain and set aside. (If using dried favas: Soak the beans in cold water for 3 to 4 hours, then slip off the tough skins. Cook in boiling salted water for about 25 minutes, until softened but not split.) Wash and peel the carrots, cutting off all but a couple inches of the tops. Blanch in boiling water for 4 minutes, plunge into cold water, drain, and set aside. Wash and trim the baby onions, leaving a couple inches of the tops. Blanch in boiling water for 6 minutes, drain, and set aside. (If using pearl onions, blanch for 6 minutes, then slip the outer layer of skin off.)

Finely chop the basil and put in a bowl with the bread crumbs, egg yolk, and $\frac{1}{2}$ cup of the butter. Use a fork to mash the ingredients together to form a uniform paste. Season lightly with salt and pepper. Divide the mixture into 4 portions, place each on a piece of plastic wrap, cover with another piece of plastic wrap, and roll out to a thickness of a little less than $\frac{1}{4}$ inch (large enough to wrap the pieces of lamb). Place in the refrigerator until firm, about 15 minutes. Wrap the lamb pieces in the bread crumb crust and set aside.

Preheat the oven to 400° F. Heat 1 tablespoon of the butter in a large ovenproof nonstick sauté pan or a well-seasoned skillet over medium-high heat. Add the lamb pieces and cook, carefully turning once, until the crust is golden brown, about 3 minutes on each side. Put the pan in the oven and roast for 6 minutes for medium-rare.

Meanwhile, brown half of the lamb bones and trimmings in a skillet over high heat. Remove and discard the bones and drain off the fat. Return the skillet to medium-high heat, pour in the stock and add the thyme, scraping up any browned bits on the bottom of the skillet. Lower the heat to maintain a simmer and cook for 15 minutes. Strain through a fine-mesh sieve and season to taste with salt and pepper; set aside.

Remove the lamb from the oven and let rest for 3 to 4 minutes. Arrange on individual serving plates. In a saucepan bring 2 cups water to a boil, add the vegetables and cook for 1 minute to reheat, then drain and arrange the vegetables around the lamb. Stir the remaining 1 tablespoon butter into the thyme sauce and spoon the sauce over the vegetables; serve immediately.

NOTE: To make the lamb stock, brown half of the lamb bones in a soup pot over high heat, then add enough water to cover the bones by about 1 inch, 2 bay leaves, 1 tablespoon peppercorns, and the carrot and onion tops. Bring to a boil, then lower the heat and simmer for 1 hour. Strain and let cool. Skim off the fat.

clay-baked rabbit
with garlic and herbs

THIS RUSTIC, FARMHOUSE RECIPE FROM THE HEART OF BORDEAUX is easy to prepare and dramatic to serve. Anne Néel, owner with her husband, Fabrice, of Château Lamothe, where they produce terrific red and white wines with the Premières-Côtes de Bordeaux appellation, makes this recipe in a red clay pot that she seals with a thick paste of flour and water. An old family recipe that's a favorite with the Néel's many friends, the dish can also be made with chicken. Rabbit, like chicken, is a very neutral meat, and absorbs the flavors of the garlic and the herbs while it cooks sealed in the pot. It also becomes very tender. The garlic cloves, which you open one by one as you eat, become sweet and creamy, and are delicious either with the rabbit, or spread on a piece of crusty country bread. The dish is excellent accompanied by sautéed potatoes and green beans or braised endive. You will need a Romertopf-style red clay pot for this recipe. Start the recipe several hours ahead to allow the rabbit time to marinate with the garlic and herbs.

3 tablespoons olive oil

One 3- to 4-pound rabbit, cut into pieces

30 cloves garlic, unpeeled

3 sprigs thyme

2 sprigs rosemary

2 sprigs tarragon

$\frac{1}{2}$ teaspoon salt

$\frac{1}{4}$ teaspoon freshly ground black pepper

1 cup flour

In a large skillet, warm the oil over medium-high heat. Add the rabbit pieces and brown thoroughly on each side, then transfer to a clay casserole. Add the garlic cloves, thyme, rosemary, tarragon, salt, and pepper to the casserole. Cover with plastic wrap, put on the top of the casserole, and refrigerate for at least 2 hours to allow the flavors to infuse the meat.

Half an hour before cooking, remove the casserole from the refrigerator, remove and discard the plastic wrap, and set aside. Preheat the oven to 350° F.

In a small bowl, combine the flour with about $\frac{1}{3}$ cup of water, and stir to create a soft dough that will be the "paste" that seals the two halves of the casserole together. Line the rim of the bottom half of the casserole with a thick "cushion" of dough, then press the top half down on it, making sure the casserole is completely sealed all around. Bake in the center of the oven for 2 hours. Bring the casserole to the table, break the seal in front of your guests, and serve.

marinated veal stew
with parsleyed dumplings

OREGANO, THYME, SAGE, AND PARSLEY flavor this succulent, aromatic veal stew. You can prepare this dish without the dumplings if you prefer, and serve it instead with buttered noodles. But I love dumplings, especially these, flecked with parsley, and add them to most stews to cook in the fragrant steam just before serving.

SERVES 4 TO 6

For the Stew

6 tablespoons olive oil

2 tablespoons freshly squeezed lemon juice

1 tablespoon white wine vinegar

3 cloves garlic, halved and crushed

Salt

Freshly ground black pepper

2 pounds shoulder or breast of veal,
    cut into 2-inch cubes

1 teaspoon coarsely chopped oregano or marjoram

1 teaspoon coarsely chopped thyme

2 sage leaves, finely julienned

5 tablespoons chopped parsley

4 celery leaves, finely julienned

1 medium onion, chopped

2 ounces slab bacon, cut into $1/2$-inch cubes

1 cup dry white wine, such as Sauvignon Blanc
    or Chardonnay

2 cups veal or chicken stock

2 medium carrots, cut into $1/4$-inch slices

3 tablespoons unsalted butter

4 tablespoons flour

For the Dumplings

1 cup milk

1 tablespoon unsalted butter

2 cups flour

1 tablespoon baking powder

$1/3$ cup chopped parsley

$1/2$ teaspoon salt

Parsley springs for garnish

Begin the stew: In a large glass or ceramic bowl, combine 3 tablespoons of the oil, the lemon juice, vinegar, garlic, salt, and pepper to taste, and whisk to combine. Add the veal and stir with a wooden spoon to coat the veal with the marinade. Add the oregano, thyme, sage, 3 tablespoons of the parsley, the celery leaves, and onion, and stir to combine. Cover the bowl and refrigerate for 3 to 6 hours, stirring from time to time to keep the veal pieces evenly coated with the marinade. Remove the bowl from the refrigerator about 30 minutes before cooking.

In a large skillet, heat the remaining 3 tablespoons

of oil over medium heat. Remove the pieces of veal from the marinade, add them in batches to the oil, and stir. Cook the veal just long enough for the pieces to color lightly on all sides, but not brown, about 2 minutes; you want to gently seal in the juices, but not sear or cook them through. Transfer the veal to a large casserole or Dutch oven. Add the bacon to the skillet and cook until the pieces are light golden brown, then add them to the casserole. Add all the ingredients from the marinade to the casserole, then add the wine, stock, and $\frac{1}{2}$ teaspoon salt, and stir to combine. Bring the mixture to a boil over high heat, then lower the heat to medium-low, cover, and cook, stirring occasionally so the veal doesn't stick to the bottom of the pot, for 45 minutes. Stir in the carrots and cook for 45 minutes longer.

Meanwhile, make the dumplings: In a saucepan, combine the milk and butter, and gently warm over medium-low heat until the butter melts. Remove from the heat. In a mixing bowl, combine the flour, baking powder, parsley, and salt. Add the milk mixture to the dry ingredients and stir in, or mix with your hands, until a soft dough forms. Set aside.

Then, in a saucepan, melt the butter over medium-low heat. Sprinkle in the flour, whisking constantly to make a roux, or smooth paste. Ladle about $\frac{1}{2}$ cup of the hot broth from the casserole into the pan and whisk briskly to blend and thicken the broth. Set aside.

After the carrots have cooked in the veal mixture for 45 minutes, stir the thickened broth in the saucepan. Pour the broth back into the casserole, stirring until the veal mixture thickens. Adjust the seasoning, then drop the dumpling dough, a heaping tablespoon at a time, onto the top of the bubbling veal mixture. Cover and cook, without lifting the cover, for 15 minutes. Remove from the heat, then spoon the stew and dumplings into warmed bowls or soup plates, garnish with parsley, and serve immediately.

spiced island pork stew
with sage, cilantro, and coconut

THIS IS A LUSCIOUS and tender pork stew, redolent with sage, marjoram, and undertones of sherry, and slightly sweet from the addition of coconut milk. The garnish of cilantro and toasted coconut imparts an exotic finishing touch typical of tropical island fare, whether it be Tahiti, Mauritius, or deep in the Grenadines. The recipe was inspired by a packet of spices my husband, Steve, brought home with him from the Caribbean island of Grenada—nicknamed "The Spice Island"—and his recounting of several delicious meals he had during his visit. I serve this with long-grain rice cooked in chicken broth with a handful of golden raisins, and a delectably bitter watercress and endive salad with a lemon-Dijon vinaigrette.

SERVES 4 TO 6

5 tablespoons olive oil

2 tablespoons freshly squeezed lemon juice

1 clove garlic, crushed and minced

3 tablespoons soy sauce

3 sage leaves, minced

3 pounds pork loin or shoulder,
  cut into stew-size cubes

3 tablespoons medium-dry sherry,
  such as Amontillado

2 tablespoons cornstarch

2 tablespoons brown sugar

1 cup chicken broth

½ cup coconut milk

½ teaspoon chopped marjoram

¼ teaspoon each of: ground nutmeg, ground
  ginger, and ground cloves

Freshly ground black pepper

1¼ cups cilantro, coarsely chopped

1¼ cups shredded and toasted coconut

1 cup dry-roasted peanuts, chopped

In a small bowl, combine 4 tablespoons of the oil, the lemon juice, garlic, 1 tablespoon of the soy sauce, and the sage, and whisk to combine; this is the marinade. Place the pork cubes in a large glass or ceramic bowl, and pour the marinade over. Mix with a large wooden spoon or your hands, turning the meat over and over until it is thoroughly coated with marinade. Cover with plastic wrap and refrigerate for 1 to 2 hours.

Preheat the oven to 375° F. In a large skillet, heat the remaining tablespoon oil over medium-high heat. Working in batches, remove the pork cubes from the marinade, add to the pan, and brown until they are lightly golden on each side. Transfer the pork to a heavy-bottomed enamel casserole, pour in any remaining marinade from the bowl, and set aside.

In a medium mixing bowl, combine the remaining

2 tablespoons soy sauce, the sherry, and cornstarch, and stir to dissolve the cornstarch. Add the brown sugar, chicken broth, coconut milk, marjoram, spices, and several turns of the pepper mill, and mix with a wire whisk until all the ingredients are blended and the sugar dissolved. Pour over the pork and stir to combine thoroughly. Over medium-high heat, bring the pork mixture to a boil, cover, then transfer to the oven and bake for 2 hours, stirring once or twice.

Remove from the oven, stir in $\frac{1}{4}$ cup of the cilantro and $\frac{1}{4}$ cup of the toasted coconut, cover again, and set aside for 5 minutes. Transfer to a warmed, deep-sided serving dish and garnish with a bit of the remaining cilantro and coconut; put the rest of the cilantro and coconut into small serving dishes, along with the peanuts. Serve immediately, passing the dishes of cilantro, coconut, and peanuts at the table.

veal saltimbocca

THIS TRADITIONAL ITALIAN DISH, easy to prepare and quick to cook, originated in the town of Brescia. It's name literally means "jump into the mouth." The tangy, spicy sage adds delicious contrast to the richness of the veal, prosciutto, and mozzarella. You can also make this dish with ultra-thin slices of chicken scallopine. Serve it with buttered, parsleyed spaghetti.

SERVES 4

8 veal scallopine slices, 2 to 3 ounces each, pounded to thickness of $\frac{1}{8}$ inch

2 ounces paper-thin prosciutto slices

Freshly ground black pepper

$\frac{1}{2}$ cup finely shredded mozzarella

8 sprigs sage, 3 to 4 leaves each

4 tablespoons unsalted butter

2 tablespoons olive oil

1 cup dry white wine, such as Chardonnay

1 teaspoon finely minced sage

Sea salt

2 tablespoons minced parsley

Cover the veal slices with slices of prosciutto, trimming prosciutto or folding it to fit. Season with a few turns of the pepper mill, sprinkle with the mozzarella, then lay the sage sprigs in the center of each slice. Fold the slices in half and secure each packet with a toothpick.

In a large skillet over medium-high heat, heat 2 tablespoons of the butter and the oil until bubbling. Add the veal and cook until lightly browned on one side, then turn and cook until lightly browned on the other side. As they cook, baste them with the butter mixture. Transfer to a warmed serving plate and keep warm in a very low oven. Add the wine to the skillet and bring to a boil over medium-high heat, scraping up any browned bits on the bottom of the pan. Lower the heat to medium and cook until the mixture is reduced by half. Stir in the remaining butter, the minced sage, and salt to taste, and cook for 1 minute. Remove from the heat. Arrange 2 veal packets on each of 4 serving plates. Remove the toothpicks. Spoon the sauce over the veal, garnish with parsley, and serve immediately.

desserts
and
beverages

chocolate-thyme charlotte

THE STOHRER PÂTISSERIE, FOUNDED IN 1725, is the oldest pastry shop in Paris, making exquisite pastries that have been seducing Parisians since the days of Louis XV. The original Chef Stohrer was, in fact, the pastry chef to Louis XV at Versailles before striking out on his own to open a pastry shop on the rue Montorgeuil in Paris. The shop, still in the same spot, with a deep blue façade and bright yellow awnings, is a classified historic monument. Stohrer's pastries are as sublime in taste as they are beautiful to gaze upon. In this recipe—demanding, labor-intensive, and not, perhaps, for the inexperienced cook—two layers of intensely flavored chocolate cake sandwich a creamy layer of thyme-flavored Bavarian cream, the ensemble topped by a thick crown of chocolate mousse. It's an extraordinary dessert worth the effort that goes into it.

SERVES 8

For the Chocolate Cake Layers

2 ounces almond paste

$\frac{1}{2}$ cup sugar

2 eggs, lightly beaten

4 egg whites

2 tablespoons flour

2 tablespoons cocoa powder

1 ounce (1 square) semisweet chocolate

$1\frac{1}{2}$ tablespoons unsalted butter

For the Thyme Bavaroise

1 cup crème fraîche

$\frac{1}{3}$ cup plus 1 tablespoon sugar

1 tablespoon thyme leaves

One $\frac{1}{4}$-ounce packet unflavored gelatin

4 egg yolks

1 cup heavy cream, whipped

For the Chocolate Mousse

7 ounces (7 squares) semisweet
  chocolate, very finely chopped

$\frac{3}{4}$ cup plus 2 tablespoons crème fraîche

$\frac{3}{4}$ cup heavy cream, whipped

About 1 cup shaved semisweet or dark chocolate

Make the chocolate cake layers: Mix the almond paste with $\frac{1}{4}$ cup of the sugar, then add, little by little, the beaten eggs, mixing constantly, and blend until smooth; set aside. In a mixing bowl, beat the egg whites, adding the remaining sugar little by little, until you get firm peaks.

Preheat the oven to 350° F. Line the bottoms of two 8-inch cake pans with circles of kitchen parchment. Sift the flour and the cocoa together into a small bowl; set aside. In a small saucepan over very low heat, melt the semisweet chocolate and butter. Transfer to a mixing bowl and fold in about 1 cup of the egg white mixture, folding until it is smooth. Add the almond paste mixture and stir to combine. Add the cocoa-flour mixture and stir to combine. Finally, gently fold in the remaining egg white mixture one-third at a time, maintaining as much volume as possible. Pour the mixture into the prepared cake pans and cook until the cakes are firm on top and have pulled away from the sides, about 20 minutes. Set aside on wire racks to cool.

Make the thyme bavaroise: In a small saucepan over medium heat, combine the crème fraîche and half the sugar and stir to combine. Bring to a boil, then remove from the heat, stir in the thyme, and set aside for 10 minutes to infuse.

Sprinkle the gelatin over $\frac{1}{4}$ cup cold water and set aside. In a mixing bowl, combine the egg yolks and the remaining sugar and beat until pale yellow. Transfer to a clean saucepan. Strain the thyme mixture through a fine-mesh sieve into a small bowl and discard the thyme. Stirring constantly, pour the thyme-infused cream into the egg yolk mixture and heat to just below boiling, 185° F on a candy thermometer; take care that the mixture does not brown on the bottom. (If you accidentally scrape up browned bits, after it reaches the correct temperature, strain through a sieve lined with a layer of cheesecloth.) Remove from the heat, transfer to a mixing bowl, then add the gelatin and stir to blend

thoroughly. Cover the surface with plastic wrap and set aside to cool. Fold in the whipped cream, cover with plastic wrap, and refrigerate.

Make the chocolate mousse: Place the chopped chocolate in a mixing bowl and set aside. In a small saucepan over medium heat, bring the crème fraîche to a boil. Remove from the heat, then pour half over the chocolate, stirring to melt the chocolate. Pour the remaining cream over the chocolate and stir to combine. Set aside to cool completely. Carefully fold about 1 cup of the whipped cream into the chocolate mixture, then fold in the remaining whipped cream one-third at a time, maintaining as much volume as possible. Cover with plastic wrap and refrigerate.

Assemble the charlotte: Turn one layer of the chocolate cake out onto a cake plate covered with a doily; peel off the parchment. Spread the thyme bavaroise over the cake, spreading to the edges. Place the second layer of cake over the bavaroise, pressing slightly until the bavaroise is flush with the outside of the cake layers; peel off the parchment. Spread on the chocolate mousse, smoothing it to the edges, then smooth the sides with a palette knife so that the mousse forms a distinct fourth layer. Garnish the top generously with shaved chocolate and refrigerate until ready to serve. Serve within 3 hours.

crème brûlée with lavender

THIS RICH AND UNCTUOUS CRÈME BRÛLÉE, made with crème fraîche and delicately perfumed with fresh lavender, comes from Didier Schneiter, Executive Chef of the spectacular Beau Rivage Palace Hotel on the shores of Lake Geneva in Lausanne, Switzerland.

SERVES 4

2 cups crème fraîche

3 sprigs lavender (flowered portions only)

6 large egg yolks

⅓ cup granulated sugar

⅓ cup brown sugar

½ pint fresh berries, such as raspberries, blackberries, or blueberries (optional)

4 tiny bouquets of fresh lavender (optional)

Place the crème fraîche in a small saucepan and heat gently over medium heat until it just reaches a simmer. Remove from the heat and stir in the lavender sprigs. Set aside for 10 to 15 minutes to infuse. Strain the crème fraîche into a large bowl, discarding the lavender.

Fill a medium saucepan one-third full of hot water and place over high heat to bring to boil. Lower the heat to maintain a simmer. In a medium bowl, whisk the egg yolks to loosen. While whisking, add the granulated sugar in a stream. Place the bowl over the simmering water in the saucepan and whisk constantly until the yolks are warm. Add the yolk mixture to the crème fraîche and whisk together gently. Pour into four 6-ounce molds, and place in a large roasting pan. Set aside until the oven is heated. Meanwhile, fill the saucepan with water and bring to a boil.

Preheat the oven to 300° F. Place the rack in the center of the oven and pull out slightly. Place the roasting pan with filled molds on the rack, then pour boiling water into the roasting pan so that water comes halfway up the sides of the molds. Carefully slide the pan into the oven and close the door. Bake for 45 min-

utes to 1 hour, until the custard is almost set, but still slightly jiggly in the center. Begin checking after 40 minutes, as ovens vary. When done, remove the molds from the water bath and place on a wire rack to cool completely. (The custards may be refrigerated at this point for up to two days.)

When the custards are cooled, preheat the broiler, or have on hand a home-sized blow torch. Blot any moisture off the custards with a dry paper towel, then sprinkle them evenly with the brown sugar, about 1 generous tablespoon each. Place them under the broiler so that the tops are about 2 inches from the heat source. Broil until the sugar on the top is bubbling, then becomes a deep golden brown. Watch them carefully, and rotate as necessary. The browning over the surface may be slightly uneven, but that's fine. If you're using a home blow torch, use medium-high heat and direct the flame onto the sugared surface, waving the flame over the area. Let the crème brûlées rest briefly for the sugar to become crisp, then place them on a plate and surround them with berries and sprigs of lavender, if desired. Serve warm.

riviera spiced peach salad
with basil

THIS FRAGRANT SPICED PEACH SALAD WITH BASIL was created by Christian Willer, Executive Chef of the legendary Hotel Martinez in Cannes. It is a favorite dessert in the hotel's glamorous art deco restaurant, Le Palme D'Or.

SERVES 6

½ cup sugar

2 cinnamon sticks

1 whole vanilla bean

2 whole cloves

20 basil leaves

6 large, ripe but firm peaches, peeled (see note)

2 tablespoons unsalted butter

½ cup sliced almonds

3 tablespoons crème de cassis or black currant liqueur (optional)

6 sprigs basil

In a large saucepan, combine 2 cups water with the sugar, cinnamon, vanilla bean, cloves, and basil leaves, and bring to a boil over medium-high heat. Place the peaches in the syrup, lower the heat to medium-low, and cook, basting the peaches frequently, for 5 minutes. Set aside and allow the peaches to cool in the mixture.

Remove the peaches from the syrup; cover the syrup with plastic wrap and reserve in the refrigerator. Slice the peaches in half, remove the pits, then slice each half into four sections. Cover the peach sections with plastic wrap and refrigerate for about 1 hour. Just before serving, melt the butter in a small skillet over medium-high heat. Add the almonds, stir to coat them with butter, and cook until the almonds are golden brown, about 4 minutes. Strain the reserved syrup into a small bowl. Stir in the liqueur, if you wish. Arrange the peach sections decoratively, perhaps in a pinwheel design, on 6 serving plates, one peach per plate. Spoon the syrup over the peaches, sprinkle with the almonds, and garnish with a basil sprig. Serve immediately.

NOTE: To peel peaches, blanch them for 30 seconds in boiling water, drain, transfer to a bowl of cold water, and slip off the skins.

tarragon liqueur

THIS IS AN OLD-FASHIONED FRENCH COUNTRY RECIPE from Aude Kamlet, an artist who divides her time between Touraine, in her native France, and a home in New York. An after-dinner drink the French call a *digestif,* literally a beverage to aid digestion after a big meal, this sweet, tarragon-infused liqueur has a pleasant aniselike flavor, but it is perhaps not for every taste; some people may find it a bit pharmaceutical. It takes six weeks to infuse.

MAKES 1 $\frac{1}{2}$ QUARTS

1 large bunch tarragon, washed, patted dry, stems discarded
(you should have about 2 ounces of leaves)
1 $\frac{1}{2}$ quarts vodka
1 cup sugar
3 or 4 drops vanilla extract

Combine the tarragon leaves and the vodka in a 2-quart glass container. Seal tightly, then store in a dark, cool place for 3 weeks. Strain out the tarragon leaves, return the vodka to the glass container, add the sugar and the vanilla extract, seal tightly, and store in a dark, cool place for another 3 weeks. Serve in small cordial glasses at the end of a meal. Store tightly sealed. As Kamlet says, this liqueur will last forever.

baked apples stuffed
with thyme and dates

THESE SAVORY BAKED APPLES work well as an autumn dessert or as an accompaniment to a succulent roast pork or roast goose. The thyme and sage add an earthy, herbal touch to the honeyed sweetness of the dates, raisins, and apples.

SERVES 4

$^1\!/_2$ cup pitted and chopped dates

$^1\!/_2$ cup golden raisins

1 tablespoon thyme leaves, lightly crushed

$^1\!/_2$ cup plus 2 tablespoons brown sugar

2 tablespoons unsalted butter

4 sweet-tart apples like Rome Beauty or crisp Macintosh, cored and peeled halfway down

6 sprigs sage

$^1\!/_4$ cup apricot jam

Preheat the oven to 375° F. In a medium bowl, combine the dates, raisins, thyme, and 2 tablespoons of the brown sugar, and set aside. In a small saucepan, combine the remaining sugar with $^1\!/_2$ cup water and 1 tablespoon of the butter, and bring to a boil. Cook for about 5 minutes, until the mixture forms a clear golden syrup. Set aside.

Stuff the apples with the date mixture, filling them a bit over the top so they look "overstuffed." Cut the remaining 1 tablespoon butter into little bits and push them into the top of the date stuffing. Place a sprig of sage in the center of each apple, pushing it down into the date stuffing about halfway. Place the apples in a 9- by 13-inch baking pan. Pour the sugar syrup around them, and bake in the center of the oven for 45 minutes, testing for doneness every 10 minutes or so, until the apples are tender.

Remove from the oven. Combine the apricot jam with 1 teaspoon water in a small cup. Heat the mixture in a microwave oven or on the stove, stirring to combine. With a pastry brush, brush the tops and peeled sides of the apples with the apricot glaze. Return to the oven for 10 minutes. Set pan on a wire rack to cool. Remove sage sprigs, and replace, if you wish, with 2 fresh sage leaves on the top of each apple. Brush them with a bit more apricot glaze. Serve warm, at room temperature, or chilled. If serving as a dessert, place apples in individual bowls and spoon on some sugar syrup from the pan.

dark chocolate–basil tartlets

CHOCOLATE WITH BASIL MAY BE A SURPRISING COMBINATION, but the blend of flavors is intriguingly subtle. Serve these tartlets, if you wish, garnished with a bit of whipped cream and a tiny sprig of basil. For a change of pace, you can also make this recipe using white chocolate and mint instead of the basil. The texture of the white chocolate tart will be more unctuous, the flavor a bit sweeter. You will need six 4-inch, removable-bottom tartlet pans. If you don't have the time or the inclination to prepare the pastry crust from scratch, you could use miniature graham-cracker tartlet shells usually available in the baking aisle of the supermarket. Begin preparations about 5 hours ahead of serving.

MAKES 6 TARTLETS

For the Pastry Crust

$1^3/_4$ cups flour

$^1/_2$ cup unsalted butter, chilled and cut into bits

$^1/_2$ cup sugar

$^1/_4$ teaspoon salt

2 eggs, beaten

For the Filling

9 ounces (9 squares) bittersweet dark chocolate, chopped into bits

$^1/_2$ cup plus 2 tablespoons heavy cream

1 small bunch (about 1 cup loosely packed) basil

3 tablespoons unsalted butter, softened

$^1/_2$ cup whipped cream (optional)

6 small basil sprigs (optional)

Make the flaky sweet pastry crust: In the bowl of a food processor, or in a mixing bowl, combine the flour, butter, sugar, and salt, and process for about 12 seconds, or mash together with your fingertips, until the mixture is crumbly, resembling coarse sand. Add the eggs and pulse 12 to 14 times, or mix until the dough comes together but before it forms a ball. If the dough seems too sticky, add a rounded tablespoon of flour and pulse a few more times until blended. Remove the dough, form it into a ball with your hands, then press it into a flat disk between your hands. Wrap in plastic wrap and place in the refrigerator for at least 1 hour.

On a floured work surface, and using a floured rolling pin, roll out the dough to a 14-inch circle about $^1/_8$ inch thick. Using a large cup or small bowl about 5 inches in diameter, cut out 6 circles of dough. Press into six 4-inch tartlet pans and crimp the edges. Prick the bottom of the crust with a fork. Cover each with plastic wrap and refrigerate for 15 minutes.

Preheat the oven to 375° F. Remove the plastic wrap, then line the tart shells with small squares of aluminum foil. Fill the shells to the brim with dried beans or baking weights. Bake for 8 minutes, remove the beans or weights and the foil, return to the oven, and bake for 10 to 15 minutes longer, until the crust is light golden brown all over. Transfer to a wire rack to cool before filling.

Make the filling: Place the chocolate in a large Pyrex or heatproof mixing bowl and set aside. In a small saucepan, combine the cream and the basil, and bring to just below boiling over medium-high heat. Remove from the heat and let the basil infuse for 1 minute. Remove and discard the basil, then pour the cream over the chocolate, and stir to melt and combine. If chocolate does not completely melt, set the bowl over the lowest setting on the burner—so that the burner is just warm—and stir the mixture until the chocolate and cream are incorporated. Remove from the heat, add the butter, and stir to melt and incorporate. Cover the bowl loosely with plastic wrap and set aside to cool until lukewarm.

Using a small ladle or a serving spoon, fill the tartlet shells with the chocolate mixture, filling them to just below the brim. Set aside in a cool—but not cold—place for at least 4 hours. Do not refrigerate. The tart should be firm but still unctuous. Top, if you wish, with a dollop of whipped cream and a sprig of basil, and serve.

minty mary cocktail

I FIRST HAD THIS COCKTAIL ONE BLISTERING HOT AFTERNOON at a ranch in the Camargue region of southern France. After it macerated in a glass pitcher all morning, it was served in a tall glass filled with ice, garnished with mint, and liberally laced with gin. The four elements of this cocktail—tomato juice, lemons, mint, and gin—create a wonderfully refreshing and unusual potion. You can also make it with vodka, or, of course, with no alcohol at all.

SERVES 6 TO 8

6 cups (1½ quarts) tomato juice
3 lemons, sliced into rounds
1 bunch mint
8 ounces (1 cup) gin
6 to 8 lemon wedges (optional)
6 to 8 sprigs mint (optional)

In a large pitcher, combine the tomato juice, sliced lemons, and mint. Set aside to macerate for about 3 hours. When ready to serve, fill 6 to 8 tall glasses with ice. Remove and discard the mint and lemons from the pitcher. Add the gin and stir with a long wooden spoon to blend. Pour into the glasses, garnish, if you wish, with lemon wedges and sprigs of mint, and serve immediately.

fruit salad with white wine, rosemary, and sage sauce

THIS IS AN EASY, LIGHT, and refreshing fruit salad, bathed in white wine and infused with the flavors of rosemary, sage, and lemon thyme. Prepare it about an hour ahead of time to allow the salad to chill and the flavors to blend. I use a fruity white wine such as a Riesling, or occasionally, for a more exotic, opulent taste, an Alsatian Gewürztraminer.

SERVES 6

$\frac{1}{3}$ cup wildflower, or plain, liquid honey

1 sprig rosemary

1 teaspoon chopped lemon thyme or lemon verbena

2 minced sage leaves

1 cup white wine, such as Riesling, Gewürztraminer, or Chardonnay

5 cups mixed fresh fruit, such as honeydew melon, cantaloupe, pineapple, papaya, or apples cubed or shaped into balls; strawberries halved or seedless red grapes

In a bowl in a microwave oven, or in a small saucepan placed over low heat, warm the honey until it is quite fluid, but not boiling. Remove from the heat. Place the rosemary sprig, the lemon thyme, and the sage in a small mixing bowl, then pour the honey over the herbs and stir to combine. Set aside for 5 minutes. Add the wine and stir briskly with a small wire whisk to blend. Place the mixed fruit in a large glass bowl, then pour the honey mixture, including the rosemary sprig, over the fruit, and stir gently with a large mixing spoon to coat the fruit thoroughly with the sauce. Cover with plastic wrap and refrigerate for about 1 hour, stirring occasionally. Remove the plastic wrap, discard the rosemary sprig, then stir once more before ladling into chilled serving bowls, making sure that each serving has lots of sauce.

lemon verbena bread

THIS IRRESISTIBLE TEA BREAD RECIPE, contributed by the New York Unit of the Herb Society of America, gets its lemony flavor from lemon verbena and the juice and zest of a lemon. If lemon verbena is in short supply, substitute up to half the amount needed with lemon balm. If you can't obtain any fresh lemon verbena, use dried. Prepare the day before and serve at teatime or for breakfast.

SERVES 6 TO 8

For the Bread
$\frac{1}{2}$ cup unsalted butter, softened,
  plus additional for the pan
$\frac{1}{4}$ cup chopped lemon verbena leaves
1 cup sugar
2 eggs
2 cups milk
$1\frac{1}{2}$ cups flour, sifted

1 teaspoon baking powder
Salt
Grated zest of 1 lemon

For the Glaze
$\frac{1}{2}$ cup sugar
Juice of 1 lemon
2 tablespoons chopped lemon verbena leaves

Make the bread: Preheat the oven to 350° F. Grease 1 large loaf pan or 2 small loaf pans with butter. In the bowl of an electric mixer, combine the butter and the lemon verbena and mix to blend. Add the sugar, eggs, milk, flour, baking powder, a pinch of salt, and the lemon zest, and mix at medium speed until the batter is smooth and thoroughly blended. Pour the batter into the prepared pan. Bake for 35 to 40 minutes, until the top is golden brown.

Meanwhile, make the glaze: Combine the sugar, lemon juice, and lemon verbena in a small bowl and whisk to combine thoroughly.

Remove the bread from the oven and set the pan on a wire rack. Spread the glaze over the top of the bread while still hot. Let sit for several hours before removing from the pan. Wrap the bread carefully and set aside overnight to allow the flavors to develop, or wrap in freezer wrap and freeze immediately.

minted hot cocoa

THIS IS A SOUL-WARMING treat on a chilly morning, or by the fire on a dark winter's afternoon.

SERVES 4 TO 5

1 quart whole milk
1 small bunch mint
$\frac{1}{2}$ vanilla bean, or $\frac{1}{2}$ teaspoon vanilla extract
$\frac{1}{3}$ cup unsweetened cocoa
$\frac{1}{3}$ cup sugar
Whipped cream or marshmallows (optional)

In a large saucepan, heat the milk to just below the boiling point. Remove from the heat, add the mint and the vanilla bean, if using, cover the pot, and set aside for 5 minutes to infuse.

Meanwhile, in a small saucepan, combine the cocoa and sugar with $\frac{1}{2}$ cup water, and bring to a boil over high heat. Lower the heat to medium, and cook for about 2 minutes, stirring constantly, until the mixture thickens slightly into a syrup. Remove from the heat.

Remove and discard the mint and the vanilla bean from the milk. Pour in the chocolate syrup, add the vanilla extract now, if using, and stir to blend. Return to medium heat, and cook until hot. Serve immediately in mugs or cups, garnished, if you wish, with whipped cream or marshmallows.

rosemary and single-malt scotch soufflé

IN THIS INTRIGUING AND INVENTIVE RECIPE from three-star Paris chef Pierre Gagnaire, three essential ingredients—rosemary, brown sugar, and single-malt Scotch—combine to create intensely flavored lighter-than-air individual soufflés. Everything except the infused oil must be prepared just before serving (although you can, and should, have each ingredient out and ready ahead of time—yolks in one bowl, whites in another, rosemary, sugars, and Scotch measured out). Gagnaire serves this soufflé topped by a drizzle of vanilla-infused light olive oil, and accompanied by slices of sweet currant-studded brioche.

MAKES 6 TO 8 INDIVIDUAL SOUFFLÉS

7 egg yolks
1 large sprig rosemary
3 tablespoons brown sugar
2 tablespoons single-malt Scotch

10 egg whites
1/3 cup granulated sugar
2 to 3 tablespoons vanilla-infused light
olive oil (see note)

Preheat the oven to 400° F. In a medium heavy-bottomed pot, combine the egg yolks, rosemary, brown sugar, and Scotch, and whisk to blend. Place the pot over the lowest possible heat and whisk constantly until the mixture becomes pale, slightly thickened, and silky, 2 to 3 minutes. Be very careful that the egg doesn't separate and cook in little clumps; this is why the heat must be very low and the whisking must be constant. Remove from the heat, continuing to whisk for a moment so the mixture doesn't coagulate, then set aside.

In the bowl of an electric mixer, combine the egg whites and 2 tablespoons of the granulated sugar. Beat the whites on medium-high speed, adding the remaining sugar a tablespoon at a time, until the whites form medium, but not stiff, peaks.

Gently fold about 1 cup of the whites into the yolk mixture, then fold in another cup, and then one more.

Transfer the mixture back into the bowl of remaining beaten whites and fold in, maintaining as much volume as possible. Remove and discard the rosemary. Spoon the mixture into 6 to 8 individual soufflé dishes, or 4- to 5-inch ramekins or ovenproof bowls, place in the center of the oven, and bake until the soufflés puff up and turn golden brown on top, 5 to 8 minutes.

To serve, make a tiny indentation in the center of the soufflés, drizzle in 1 teaspoon of the vanilla-infused oil, and serve immediately.

NOTE: The oil must be made several days ahead. Combine 1/2 cup light or extra-light olive oil with the seeds scraped from 1/2 vanilla bean; stir to blend, cover, and set aside in a cool place until ready to use, then strain out the seeds.

citrus-mint iced tea

THIS REFRESHING AND DELICIOUS beverage is a cross between traditional iced tea and a fruit punch.

SERVES 6

1 quart brewed Darjeeling tea, cold
1 cup freshly squeezed orange juice
$\frac{1}{2}$ cup pineapple juice
Juice of 1 lemon
$\frac{1}{4}$ cup sugar, or more to taste
$\frac{1}{4}$ cup spearmint, lightly crushed
6 mint sprigs for garnish (optional)

Combine all the ingredients in a large pitcher and stir until the sugar dissolves. Cover the top of the pitcher with plastic wrap and refrigerate for at least 2 hours. Just before serving, stir well. Serve in tall glasses over ice. Garnish, if you wish, with mint sprigs.

lemon verbena-infused
chocolate mousse

FROM THE STATELY LAUSANNE PALACE HOTEL in Switzerland, and hotel Executive Chef Eric Redolat, comes this lovely summertime chocolate mousse, infused with the subtle flavor of fresh lemon verbena. The combination of chocolate with mint is traditional, the combination of chocolate with other herbs less well known. Yet chocolate takes beautifully to the addition of a variety of aromatic herbs, particularly basil, thyme, or lemon verbena. The herbs' bright notes of spice, citrus, and menthol play on the palette and enhance the flavor and richness of the chocolate.

SERVES 8

2 cups milk

1 bunch fresh lemon verbena

8 egg yolks

$^{3}/_{4}$ cup sugar

11 ounces (11 squares) semisweet chocolate, broken into pieces

$1^{1}/_{4}$ cups heavy cream

In a saucepan, heat the milk over medium heat to just below boiling. Remove from the heat, add the lemon verbena, stir, then set aside to infuse for 15 minutes. Remove and discard the lemon verbena, and set the milk aside.

In a large saucepan, whisk together the egg yolks and sugar. Heat the infused milk again to just below boiling, then pour it into the egg yolk mixture, stirring constantly with a wooden spoon. Set over medium heat and stir constantly until the sauce thickens and coats the back of the spoon; do not let the sauce come to a boil or the eggs will scramble. Remove from the heat. Add the chocolate pieces and stir until the chocolate is melted and completely incorporated into the sauce. Transfer to a mixing bowl, cover with plastic wrap, and refrigerate to cool.

Meanwhile, whip the cream until it forms firm peaks. Cover with plastic wrap and refrigerate until the chocolate mixture has cooled. Then, using a large rubber spatula, fold the whipped cream into the chocolate mixture, one-third at a time. Fold gently to maintain as much volume as possible. Transfer to a serving bowl or into individual serving dishes, cover with plastic wrap, and chill for 1 hour, or until ready to serve.

appendix

MAIL-ORDER SPECIALTY INGREDIENTS AND FOOD SOURCES

For a wide variety of olive oils, nut oils, vinegars, salts, peppers, olives, sugars, vanilla beans, and much more, contact the following companies for information or a catalog:

Balducci's
424 Avenue of the Americas
New York, NY 10011
Tel.: 800-822-1444 or 212-673-2600

Dean and Deluca
560 Broadway
New York, NY 10012
Tel.: 800-221-7714 or 212-431-1691

Maid of Scandinavia
3244 Raleigh Avenue
Minneapolis, MN 55461
Tel.: 800-328-6722 or 512-927-7966

Salumeria Italiana
1551 Richmond Street
Boston, MA 02109-1414
Tel.: 800-400-5916; Fax: 617-523-4946

For excellent fromage blanc (which freezes well so you could buy in quantity to amortize shipping costs), crème fraîche, rich cultured butter, and other dairy products:

Vermont Butter and Cheese Company
P.O. Box 95
Websterville, VT 05678
Tel.: 800-884-6287 or 802-479-9371
www.vtbutterandcheeseco.com

For a selection of goat cheese— fresh, aged, and herbed:

Little Rainbow Chèvre
Box 379 Rodham Road
Hillsdale, NY 12529
Tel.: 518-325-3351

For a broad range of domestic and imported cheeses, cut to order before shipping, as well as crème fraîche and fromage blanc:

Ideal Cheese Shop, Ltd.
1205 Second Avenue
New York, NY 10021
Tel.: 800-382-0109 or 212-688-7579

For domestic foie gras, fresh ducks, geese, and game, tasty terrines, pâtés, white truffle butter, and prepared entrées:

D'Artagnan
280 Wilson Avenue
Newark, NJ 07105
Tel.: 800-DARTAGN or 973-344-0565
www.dartagnan.com

For smoked eastern and western salmon:

Ducktrap River Fish Farm
RFD #2 Box 378
Lincolnville, ME 04849
Tel.: 207-763-3960

For succulent Maine sea scallops, Maine lobsters, excellent seasonal fish, and exclusive lines of custom-smoked salmon:

Browne Trading Company
260 Commercial Street
Portland, ME 04101
Tel.: 800-944-7848

For seasonal French produce, such as wild mushrooms, lamb's lettuce, truffles, truffle juice, and more:

Marché aux Délices
120 Imlay Street
Brooklyn, NY 11231
Tel.: 888-547-5471; Fax: 718-858-5288
www.auxdelices.com

For truffles, white truffle butter, truffle juice, canned foie gras, and caviar:

Urbani Truffles
29-24 40th Avenue
Long Island City, NY 11101
Tel.: 718-392-5050; Fax: 718-392-1704
www.urbani.com

MAIL-ORDER HERBAL PRODUCT SOURCES

For a variety of herbal products, herb plants, and herb seeds, contact the following growers and suppliers for information and catalogs:

The Cook's Garden
P.O. Box 535
Londonderry, VT 05148

The Herbfarm
32804 Issaquah-Fall City Road
Fall City, WA 98024
www.theherbfarm.com

Gilbertie's Herb Gardens
7 Sylvan Lane
Westport, CT 06880

Nichols Garden Nursery
1190 North Pacific Highway
Albany, OR 97321
www.gardennursery.com

Shepherd's Garden Seeds
30 Irene Street
Torrington, CT 06790
www.shepherdseeds.com

Wrenwood
Route 4, Box 25411
Berkeley Springs, WV 25411
www.wrenwood.com

BIBLIOGRAPHY

Anderson, Frederick O. *How to Grow Herbs for Gourmet Cooking.* New York: Meredith Press, 1967.

Bentley, Virginia Williams. *Let Herb(s) Do It.* Danville, Vermont, 1971.

Clevely, Andi, and Katherine Richmond. *The Complete Book of Herbs.* New York: Smithmark, 1994.

Darbonne, Caroline. *Le Piano d'Herbes.* Paris: Michel Lafon, 1987.

De Sounin, Leonie. *Magic in Herbs.* New York: M. Barrows and Company, 1941.

Mazza, Irma Goodrich. *Herbs for the Kitchen.* Boston: Little, Brown and Company, 1975.

New York Unit/Herb Society of America, *For Use and for Delight: A Herbal Sampler.* Kearney, Nebraska: Cookbooks by Morris Press, 2000.

Oster, Maggie, and Sal Gilbertie. *The Herbal Palette Cookbook.* Pownal, Vermont: Storey Communications, 1996.

Simmons, Adelma, and Grenier Simmons. *Herbal Harvests.* Coventry, Connecticut: Caprilands Herb Farm, 1984.

Traunfeld, Jerry. *The Herbfarm Cookbook.* New York: Scribners, 2000.

index